CIRCLING
THE
STAR

CIRCLING THE STAR

ANTHONY RELLA

GODS&RADICALS PRESS

Circling The Star

Some Rights Reserved
This entire work CC-BY-NC 4.0 Anthony Rella

ISBN: 978-0-9969877-7-6

First Printed: 1 February, 2018
by Gods&Radicals Press

Cover Design by Li Pallas
LI.PALLAS.LOVES.YOU.COM

Layout by Rhyd Wildermuth
PAGANARCH.COM

Illustrations by Alley Valkyrie
PRACTICALRABBIT.COM

Editing Team
Rhyd Wildermuth
Casandra Mae

Gods&Radicals Press
PO BOX 11850
Olympia, Washington 98508

Solidarity, bulk discount, and wholesale copies available

Contact the editors or author at
Editor@Godsandradicals.org

Or for distro contact us at
Distro@ABeautifulResistance.com

visit our site of beautiful resistance
GODSANDRADICALS.ORG

WITHIN THIS BOOK

FOREWORD FROM T. THORN COYLE----6
SEX, SELF, PASSION, PRIDE, POWER, SEX----9
SPIRIT, SEX, LOVE: SKY KISSING EARTH---21
SEX EXALTED IN LOVE---39
AIR, SELF, KNOWLEDGE: SOLVE ET COAGULA---49
SELF EXALTED IN KNOWLEDGE---69
WATER, PASSION, WISDOM: TIDES AND DEPTHS---79
PASSION EXALTED IN WISDOM---99
FIRE, PRIDE, LAW: LIVES WITH WORTH--113
PRIDE EXALTED IN LAW--133
EARTH, POWER, LIBERTY: STILLNESS AND STRENGTH--145
POWER EXALTED IN LIBERTY--165
THE END IS THE BEGINNING IS THE END--177
TERMS USED IN THIS BOOK, AND HOW--179
THANK YOU--183
ABOUT THE AUTHOR--184
ABOUT GODS&RADICALS--185

A Foreword from T. Thorn Coyle

I have often said that the Iron Pentacle is a tool of revolution and the Pearl Pentacle is a tool of evolution.

These tools, brought through by Victor Anderson, have helped many people over the years, including myself. Doing the work of the Iron and Pearl Pentacles changed my life, lending me greater balance, resilience, self-knowledge, and a deeper understanding of all the relationships around me.

You see, everything in this world, and in this cosmos, are in relationship. Our patterns of avoidance and habits of pain can keep us from recognizing these relationships. As long as we see ourselves as isolated beings, the world can feel broken, distant, confusing, and cold. Bringing ourselves closer to wholeness enables all of our relationships to flourish.

One day, we awaken and realize that we are connected to each cell in our bodies, each leaf on every tree, and the most distant star our eyes can find in the night sky. And we are connected to every human, too. And together, we can build a world based on mutuality instead of a culture intent on tearing us all apart.

Doing the work of Iron and Pearl helps us liberate ourselves, so we can better work to help others toward liberation as well. And where freedom exists, so do love and justice.

I feel grateful for the work of Iron and Pearl. My whole life is profoundly different, having encountered them. To reclaim Sex, Pride, Self, Power, and Passion is to claim our humanity. To invoke Love, Law, Knowledge, Liberty, and Wisdom is to reach a hand out to every other human alive.

It was my pleasure and honor to have been one of those who passed these powerful tools along to Anthony Rella, who, like any good magician, has made them his own. He has chased their resonances through his psyche and his physical body, and been changed.

Drawing on his years of magical practice and spiritual study, Tony blends his own devotional practice with his training in psychotherapy. The result is a deep understanding, coupled with a dash of poetry. He calls on us to open to states of wonder. To plumb our depths. To be strengthened and renewed.

These tools can change you, too, if you let them.

I hope you do. We have a chance to become healthier in spirit, body, and mind.

It is my firm belief that the more people work toward their own healing and wholeness, the better off all of our communities will be.

Tony is weaving a powerful spell in this book. I hope you take it up, take it in, and over time, I hope you make this spell your own. It is a spell of strength, ecstasy, and freedom.

The world needs this.

The world needs you.

T. THORN COYLE

... been arrested at least four times. Buy her a cup of tea or a good whisky and she'll tell you about it. Author of the alt-history urban fantasy series "The Panther Chronicles," her multiple non-fiction books include *Sigil Magic for Writers, Artists & Other Creatives*, and *Evolutionary Witchcraft*. Thorn's work appears in many anthologies, magazines, and collections. She has taught magical practice in nine countries, on four continents, and in twenty-five states.

Check out her blog and sign up for her newsletter at: http://www.thorncoyle.com

SEX, PRIDE, SELF, POWER, PASSION, SEX...

Atum rose from the vast waters of Nun upon the benben mound, the first principle of being to emerge from chaotic ground. Aching with desire, Atum made love to himself until stars of ejaculate shot from his phallus, touching the waters of Nun and forming the first worlds. From his orgasmic cry and the spit of his mouth came the winds of Shu and the moisture of Tefnut, whose lovemaking birthed the starry expanse of Nut and the fertile, recumbent ground of Geb, whose lovemaking birthed the gods. Thus the children of the gods were gifted the force of creation, the spark of life which is sex and desire.

A Brief Overview of the Pentacles

The Iron Pentacle is a tool that creates authority within one's self. The Iron Pentacle is a process of individuation, bringing one's disparate energies into wholeness, claiming one's life force and bringing it into service of the personal and transpersonal will. The points of the Pentacle are named Sex, Self, Passion, Pride, and Power.

The Iron and Pearl Pentacles come through the work of poet and mystic Victor Anderson, who with Cora Anderson transmitted teachings and practices to a number of initiates. Their initiates continued to teach and develop the practice of working with the Pentacles within their lineages. These tools have also become embedded in traditions and covens influenced by, or evolved from, the Anderson Feri Tradition.[1]

The energy of the Iron Pentacle runs internally and clockwise. The inner star's energy runs from Sex to Pride to Self to Power to Passion to Sex, while the clockwise energy runs from Sex to Self to Passion to Pride to Power.[2] In the body, the Sex point is in the head, Pride in the right foot, Self in the left hand, Power in the right hand, and Passion in the left foot.[3] Those of us without some of these appendages may experiment with sensing if our etheric bodies extend to those limbs, or simply run the energy to the furthest extremity available.

Each point connects to the other point in some way, whether through the inner star or the clockwise circle, and a change in one point affects the rest. While it is a very clean, simple form, working with the Iron Pentacle continues to deepen and become more powerful over time. In early phases of working with it, we claim the energies and work through blockages within the points. As we continue to work, we might begin to look at the lines between the points. A problem with Sex, for instance, might be rectified through working on one's Passion or Pride.

The Iron Pentacle is an energetic tool. To work with it solely in an intellectual or theoretical way, without practice, limits our capacity to truly understand its potential. We must feel its energy in our body and walk with it in the world to gain the felt sense of when these energies run well and when they are corroded and blocked. Working with it as a tool of manifestation

---

1. The Anderson Feri Tradition originate with Victor and Cora Anderson, witches who transmitted and taught their tradition to a number of initiates. These initiates have in turn taught and initiated others into the Anderson lineage, or included aspects of the tradition into differentiated traditions or communities, such as Reclaiming Witchcraft or Morningstar Mystery School. A fuller account of the history of the Iron Pentacle is available in *Magic of the Iron Pentacle* by Jane Meredith and Gede Parma.
2. In the southern hemisphere, some run the outer circle in the counter-clockwise movement.
3. This is how I learned the Pentacle, as though it is in my body facing front. Some run it with the Pentacle facing back, with Self in the right hand and Pride in the left foot, etc.

and embodiment fosters surprising changes in one's life and way of being in the world.[4]

When Iron energy runs clean, strong, and bright, the Pearl Pentacle forms. Discord and irritation spurred by Iron becomes translucent brilliance, vibrating to a higher resonance: the energies named Love, Law, Knowledge, Liberty, and Wisdom.[5] Without Iron energy, these energies become stale, oppressive, and brittle. Empty word and gesture, easily said and poorly done. Iron infuses Pearl with the vibrancy and resilience of lived experience.

- When we access the fullness of Sex, we fall deeply in Love with the world.
- When we stand in healthy Pride, our wants and needs lead us to the deeper patterns of Law.
- When we root ourselves in authentic Self, an unshakeable and certain Knowledge emerges.
- When we grow strong in our Power, we discover the Liberty of self-authority and responsibility.
- When we open ourselves to the depths of Passion, we learn a resilient and cunning Wisdom.

As the Iron Pentacle reshapes the Self, the Pearl Pentacle reshapes the Self-in-Relationship, affecting our friendships, partnerships, communities, and cultures. It is akin to the Christian notion of grace, not a thing we "do" so much as what arises as a result of our work in Iron. When first trying to play a singing bowl, the sound is inconsistent and warbly. With practice, we begin to establish the tone. Eventually our hands find the groove with ease and a clear, beautiful note fills the room, cleanses the space, calms the soul.

---

[4]. Finding a teacher who can energetically support you in working the Pentacles is well advised. Researching your nearest Reclaiming community is one path to finding a teacher, as frequently these communities offer classes on Iron and Pearl. If you want to request teaching from a Feri or Faery initiate, approach with respect.

[5]. Some Feri lines that work with Pearl use "Power" for the point named "Liberty" here, making the Iron to Pearl vibration of Power to Power.

Tools for Self-Transformation

The Pentacles are magical tools that disrupt rigid and stale patterns in our lives, free up psychic energy, and redirect that energy toward our deeper values and needs. This book will explore the tools primarily in their capacity to transform and refine the Self. There are many laudable concerns and critiques about Self-focused magical workings, fearing that it will lead to self-involvement, disregard of the gods and spirits, and disdain for the needs of others. This is a particular danger when our work becomes too focused on cultivating the ego and not bringing the ego into service.

In this work, the Pentacles are a nexus between psychology and spirituality. These two disciplines are better served when regarded as separate approaches to the human condition, with unique insights and interventions that point toward ways we can fulfill our potential. That said, the roots of "psychology" might be translated as "study of the soul." The psyche is the retina through which we experience and interpret the world. We can certainly have spiritual practice without a practice of studying our souls, but they work quite well in concert.

Michael Sebastian Lux offers an important distinction between psychology and the "sloppy thinking" he calls "psychologization," which is to assert "that everything can be reduced to projections of consciousness."[6] To illustrate this distinction, consider the following: A child grows up with caregivers, perhaps a particularly difficult caregiver that they called "Dad." The child internalizes an image of "Dad" that becomes powerfully charged and fixed in the psyche. This image was formed from how "Dad" behaved, what unconscious forces were acting through him, what the child understood about the behavior at the time, and whatever life incidents occurred that generated the emotional content and self-beliefs. How the child learns to express or not express feelings, what the child needs to feel safe, how the child relates to their needs—all of these are informed by these inner images. They become parts of the child's developing Self.

---

6. Michael Sebastian Lux, "Is 'public occultism' dying? Kicking a Dead Horse with Mr. Farrell," *Digital Enchiridon*, 19 October 2015, https://michaelseblux.wordpress.com/2015/10/19/is-public-occultism-dying-kicking-a-dead-horse-with-mr-farrell/.

As both child and parent grow, both change. Maybe the parent was irritable and punitive but begins to mellow out as an adult and regret his prior behavior. When the now-adult child is unconscious of the difference between the inner image and the outer reality, they still respond to "Dad" as though he is the internalized "Dad"—perhaps with defensiveness, resentment, or a need to please and seek validation. This extends to people who remind the child of that internalized "Dad"—spouse, bosses, teachers.

To say that "Dad" does not exist in any meaningful way except as a projection of the child's internalized image—that would be psychologizing. That would let us off the hook of being in relationship to the living people who are our parents, and we would lose much.

Yet we would lose much by neglecting those internalized images as well. Until we begin to work on our relationships with our caregivers, we do not recognize that those images are separate from the actual people, nor do we see how our reactivity co-creates the relationships we do not like. There is no capacity for distance and self-observation.

This extends to magical and spirit work. Some believe that all spirit contact is simply a psychological function, there are no entities "out there." Noncorporeal beings may interact with us through forms that seem to resemble internalized psychic images, triggering automatic responses and associations. Work on personal psychology helps us to be more flexible and resilient in our relationships and spiritual work, better able to contain that reactivity based in the past and attend to what is happening in the present moment. Internal blocks shape how we experience and interact with the world, and thus shape the world.

Work on the Self is a means to being of better service to the gods, community, and the Earth. Living a life of integrity and alignment with deep values also means experiencing a life of risk and challenge. Service, too, is joyful but demanding. Old wounds, unexpressed desires, denied dreams—unattended, they are like emotional land mines that get activated by unexpected words or circumstances and throw us off-center.

We all have our portion of emotional land mines, and the overculture tells us to "be strong," "keep it together," to ignore our vulnerabilities and plow heroically forward. Denying these weaknesses adds to the stress, and then we turn more and more toward numbing activities or lapses of integrity because "I deserve it for working so hard," and our pentacles slowly warp without our noticing.

Too often wounding leads to more wounding. Either we hurt others for triggering our emotional land mines, or we hurt ourselves to control scarier pain. Perhaps we are harmed by someone else's pride, power, passion, or sexual desire, or we are subsumed by another person's egotistical needs. We may deny these qualities in ourselves and judge others for expressing them.

We are riddled with conflicting messages about how to carry ourselves and warned about the qualities associated with the Iron Pentacle. We are supposed to be sexually desirable without liking sex too much, living authentic lives without making others uncomfortable, managing the stresses in our lives in a way that serves others' agendas for profit and productivity. These messages simultaneously devalue and overvalue sex, pride, power, passion, and self, fostering cultural complexes. Some teachers illustrate these ambivalent complexes through the Rusted (deflated) and Gilded (inflated) Pentacles.[7] Working with Rusted and Gilded is not essential, but discussing them as absences is useful for connecting with healthy Iron energy.

Bringing presence to our wounded parts generates healing. Rather than acting out pain, the practice enables us to work with it in a new way. Holding the tension of awareness and stuckness generates Pearl energy. All that discomfort and darkness the ego wants to avoid or merge becomes, with practice and presence, the raw material of Pearl. There is always a new depth to plummet, another complex to unbind, new frequencies of Iron and Pearl to discover.

The Iron Pentacle helps us to be cleaner, sharper, and stronger tools in the service of our higher calling. If you are called to serve the gods, how much more effective will you be if your emotional and physical needs are being consistently met, without needing to jump from crisis to crisis? If you

---

7. Rusted and Gilded pentacles originated from Faery initiate Steven Hewell. According to Sara Amis, Victor Anderson did not like these Pentacles, and ultimately Hewell and his line discarded their use. Others in Feri, Faery, and Reclaiming traditions do work with them.

are a vehicle for spirit communication, how much clearer a channel will you be if you are mindful of your biases and harmful inner voices? If you are an activist for justice, how much longer could you fight if you are having satisfying relationships, great sex, and feeding your soul with art you love?

Reading this Book:
A Prescriptive Practice with Choice

I have been studying witchcraft since 2005, starting with Reclaiming witchcraft, eventually moving into long-term study with T. Thorn Coyle when she was teaching Anderson Feri and continuing when she separated her teachings into Morningstar Mystery School. During this time, I also became drawn to study of the Kemetic (ancient Egyptian) pantheon.

In my early days with Reclaiming, my teachers River Roberts and Jennifer Byers mapped the Iron Pentacle points to the Western elements—correspondences that helped me to understand and work with the energies. It is as though the Elemental, Iron, and Pearl Pentacles are different resonances of the same core energies. Some compare this to the same notes played an octave apart. The particular associations of Elements to points offer deep teachings. Associating Water with Passion, for example, yields a different experience of the point than the typical association with Fire.

These particular Elemental associations are not essential or universal, and indeed some teachers even map points of the Pearl Pentacle to different points of Iron than what is presented in this book. Rather than get caught up on who has the "correct" teachings, let us consider another possibility.

In his essay "The Real Story on the Chakras," writer and yogi Hareesh, or Christopher Wallis, interrogates the Western understanding of the chakras as a coherent system of seven energy centers that have consistent associations.[8] He notes that there are many variations of chakra systems, ranging from five to more than twenty-eight, all depending upon the specific prac-

---

8. Christopher Willis, "The Real Story of the Chakras," *Tantric Studies*,
   http://tantrikstudies.squarespace.com/blog/2016/2/5/the-real-story-on-the-chakras.

tice being enacted. He suggests that none of the chakra systems are more "right" than the others, but that they were created to enact specific changes in human energy bodies. He describes the chakra systems as *prescriptive* rather than *descriptive*—that is, one is "prescribed" a particular chakra practice to bring about a specific, intended change.

Hareesh suggests that in a sense we "implant" our energy bodies with these chakras, as opposed to discovering chakras that are already there in each human. This suggests that our subtle bodies are fluid and responsive enough that they would produce appropriate imagery and energy pathways based on the system we implant.

We can explore this idea within the framework of the Triple Soul. Sticky One—the animal part of our soul—is playful, imaginative, emotional, and loves working with symbols. When we give it the idea of an energy center known as the "heart chakra," the animal part responds by creating a functioning symbolic interface. Perhaps it's an image of a bright green heart, or of a vibrant wheel, something that intuitively makes sense to this part. What might have otherwise been inchoate energies now have a specific form and function. Shining Body—the human or rational part of our soul—intellectually conceptualizes and understands the symbolic language, and is thus able to better communicate with Sticky One. God Soul, Sacred Dove, or Sacred Falcon—the divine part of our soul—too utilizes this symbolic language and energetic experience for communication. Thus we create an internal and communal frame to work with those energetic qualities, such as love, relationship, balance, the color green, and social identity.[9] Infusing the heart chakra with the Air element engenders a particular energetic expression of the chakra, a specific change in personality, but not an essential one. We could try putting Fire or Earth energy in the heart chakra to see what would happen.

---

9. These associations are taken from Anodea Judith's *Eastern Body, Western Mind*. I acknowledge that Hareesh's article criticizes Judith's approach as one of the "descriptivist" texts counter to his understanding of the intent of the chakras.

The qualities of the Pentacles may be similar, not intrinsically attached to our body parts or the elements. We might not have a latent "Pentacle" inside of us, but rather working this energy establishes and reifies the coherent internal system that, as a result, changes the Self. The tool brings these energies into a new pattern, burns away blockages, balances them, and focuses them into a clarity and purpose that would not have existed otherwise. Hence the need to run this energy regularly to maintain it, and the need to work on each point to make space for its healthy functioning.

In this book, there are several prescriptive approaches utilized that are not universally practiced by people who work with the Pentacles. These include elemental associations, Kemetic associations, and the connecting junctures between points. Each chapter is organized around a particular set of associations. First, I focus on the Iron point with an elemental association and its relationship with the other Iron points. Then I explore the Pearl resonance.

All of these workings are framed by the stories and energetic supports of certain Kemetic gods that came forward during the writing for this purpose. When I came upon the creation story of Atum, retold above, I marveled at its similarities to the Feri story of the star goddess making love to hirself and birthing the cosmos with desire. In my relationships with Kemetic deities, I experience them to be interested and supportive of this work, and I offer these associations to help frame and deepen your work with the Pentacles. You might be unwilling or unable to work with Kemetic imagery and deities. That is fine. It is not necessary.

A prescriptive practice of this sort creates a specific kind of outcome: a person whose personality has a more watery sense of Passion, for example. You may find, after trying out the associations I offer, that you wish to try different associations. Ultimately, each of us runs our own unique Iron Pentacle, and the work that comes through us as a result will be distinct.

Circling The Star

To begin, here is a practice for running the Pentacles:[10]

To run the Iron Pentacle, stand or lay down with your limbs spread out like a five-pointed star. If your body cannot do this easily or comfortably, find a posture that for you approximates the star. With a breath, imagine sending a root down into the earth, winding down until it connects with the molten core. Breathe, imagining you can pull hot red Iron energy up through your root, gathering it in the cauldron of your center, between your navel and pelvis.

When your center is full, breathe that Iron energy up into your head. Let it fill your head, noticing how this energy inhabits this point. Call out, "Sex. Sex. Sex." Breathe the energy down your neck, down the right side of your torso, through your right leg until it fills your right foot. Notice how the energy inhabits your foot. Call out, "Pride. Pride. Pride."

Breathe the energy back up your leg, across your sex, up through the left side of your torso, through your left arm, into your left hand. Notice how the energy inhabits your hand. Call out, "Self. Self. Self." Breathe the energy across your arm, through your heart and lungs, into your right hand. Notice how the energy inhabits your hand. Call out, "Power. Power. Power."

Breathe the energy through your right arm, down your torso into your left leg, down your leg, gathering in your left foot. Notice how the energy inhabits your foot. Call out, "Passion. Passion. Passion." Breathe the energy back up the left side of your body, up through your neck, back into your head. "Sex."

Move the energy through this star pattern at least three times. "Sex. Pride. Self. Power. Passion. Sex." Back in Sex, imagine that God Hirself draws the circle of Iron energy from Sex to Self to Passion to Pride to Power and back to Sex. Follow the energy through this circle pattern at least three times. "Sex. Self. Passion. Pride. Power. Sex."

If you are new to the Iron Pentacle, work with this energetic practice daily while you work through this book. Let Iron melt down impediments while you work to integrate the energies into your life.

---

10. Other guided descriptions of running the energy of the Iron and Pearl Pentacles are available in Meredith and Parma's *Magic of the Iron Pentacle* and Coyle's *Evolutionary Witchcraft*.

After you have some practice running the Iron Pentacle, you can try letting the energies resonate up to the Pearl Pentacle. After running the star and circle energy, imagine the energy moving faster, brighter, and hotter between the points, until it moves so fast that you cannot keep up.

Now imagine beautiful, soothing, pearlescent energy enfolding each Iron point and the connecting lines between. Call out the name of the Pearl points: "Love. Law. Knowledge. Liberty. Wisdom." Notice where the Pearl energy feels in relationship to your body and the Iron Pentacle. When you've run Pearl three times and return to Love, let God Hirself draw the circle again three times. "Love. Knowledge. Wisdom. Law. Liberty."

Blessed be the Iron and Pearl Pentacles.

Spirit, Sex, Love: Sky Kissing Earth

Winter Solstice: The spark of Re feels distant, having withdrawn deep inside the womb and tomb of Nut. Blessed, expansive darkness, rich black skin bejeweled with the shining souls of the justified ancients, Nut nurtures the Re within as he purifies himself of the old. Alive with power and passion, Nut stretches over the body of her beloved Geb, opening herself to him as his evergreen cock lifts from the earth, rises up in longing to connect with the ineffable cosmos. The lust of Geb, coursing with earthy ankh, becomes entwined with the lust of Nut, gathering in his passion and his semen to charge and vivify the depleted Re.

This act is the key. During the longest night, Nut's dominion, the joining of earth and sky renews the cycle of life and daylight for another. Geb unlocks the gates of Nut, and Re may be reborn.

Sex is life force. Sex is creation and creativity, sensation and pleasure, merging and separation. Sex is casual and intense. Sex crosses the abyss between beings. Sex opens the portal between the worlds. Sex is creativity, beginning with the most fundamental act of procreation.

Sex transforms. Sex generates. Sex dissolves.

The act of sex with others draws on an instinct to connect and merge, to give and receive pleasure, to momentarily loosen the boundaries of ego.

With every birth, whether it is child or creative project, that offspring separates out to become its own entity.

The Iron Pentacle begins and ends with Sex.

Spirit and Sex

The Pentacle is a symbol of the human being. Each point represents the five extremities of the human body as well as the five physical senses. The points of the Pentacle represent elements of life: Air, Fire, Water, Earth, and Spirit. When pointed upward, the Pentacle evokes the ascension of Matter toward Spirit, as in sacrifice, consecration, and death. Pointed downward, the Pentacle evokes the descent of Spirit into Matter, as in creation and birth. The language of "ascent" and "descent" comes from the Neoplatonic separation of the manifest world from the idealized world. Even within that framework, there is a mystery about the relationship between Spirit and Earth. The key to this mystery is the Pentacle, which symbolizes both.

Humans live in the friction of paradox. We are social creatures who also conceive of ourselves as individuals. We are capable of personal growth and evolution, greater self-responsibility, and yet within us is also the part of us that remembers with longing being wholly dependent, wholly a part of a greater being. We know that some day our bodies will die and our consciousnesses will go—somewhere. Perhaps to be reabsorbed into that greater being. We vacillate between the desire for autonomy, the fear of isolation, the desire for connection, and the fear of engulfment.[11]

And there, at the heart of those tensions, is Sex.

Sex is the point through which Spirit enters the manifest world and enlivens matter, discovering in turn the fulfillment of its expression. The sundering of Sex from Spirit is one of the deep wounds of modern culture. Sexual liberation looked upon the excessively rigid structures of sexuality and saw them as too restrictive and superstitious to be of value. Loosening these expectations has coincided with the blooming of gender liberation and queerness, and it has also made us vulnerable to our sexuality being

---

11. Paris Williams, *Rethinking Madness: Towards a Paradigm Shift in Our Understanding and Treatment of Psychosis* (San Rafael: Sky's Edge, 2012).

used against us. Forgetting our basic connection to life force, meaning, and Spirit through our sexuality, we believe we need to receive these gifts from the outside. Advertisers and politicians use our fears and desires around sex to sell us possessions, experiences, and legislation that only leave us further depleted and dependent.

Some argue that Spirit and Matter are wholly separate, and Matter a degraded state of being that those enspirited beings must strive to overcome to return to the godhead. When this is viewed as a sorrow, sex and reproduction are considered vices of the animal body, a drive that keeps bringing more life into the fallen world. Others who reject this doctrine argue that there is no difference between Spirit and Matter. Sex is already exalted, a celebration of the incarnate state and a proliferation of life and spirit on earth. My perspective is that there is a distinction between Spirit and Matter, yet these two states of being are themselves lovers who are in a process of separation and merging.

The gods Nut and Geb express this relationship. At night, Nut's body descends upon the recumbent Geb and the two come together in lust and love. Nut is a star goddess, a transcendent totality of being who is both womb and tomb to life, birthing Re the life-giver each morning. Geb is a green god, who gathers in the power of Re and the offspring of Nut and provides immanent home, succor, nourishment, and space to thrive. Both are necessary, both are beloved to each other, one is not superior to the other. This model of partnership offers a world-affirming, life-enhancing expression of the Neoplatonic model of separation.

By day, their parent Shu holds the two apart, enabling the existence of life. In this way, Shu corresponds to the atmosphere around the Earth, that permeable membrane between Earth and space. Without this separation, life could not thrive. Shu also corresponds to the separation of night sky and earth which allows the life-giving principle of Re to cross the horizon and bestow his ankh (life-force). The body of Shu serves in the function of the Tree of Life, separating and bridging the realms of above and below.

Witch and writer Sara Amis speaks for an enspirited world, arguing that the human problem is one of consciousness: "I would emphasize and re-emphasize that we live in a speaking world, and it will talk to us if we just shut up long enough."[12] Humans minimize our opportunities for contact with spirit and wonder, and dismiss those moments that pass through the defenses. We fall into disenchantment and unconsciousness. Sex in this state becomes a mechanical release or something to feed the ego. Even so, repetitive and desperate sexual behaviors suggest a buried dream for the deep, powerful orgasm, the transformative energy of Spirit.

The points of Spirit and Sex align when the Elemental and Iron Pentacles are stacked upon each other. Eros is a cosmic force wielded by the gods themselves. In witchcraft, sexual energy is sacred, and all consensual expressions are included—as expressed in the words written in the Charge of the Goddess, "all acts of love and pleasure are my rituals."[13] Poet and mystic Victor Anderson prays to the goddess Mari to learn to "Accept from wife or harlot the chalice, / Taking as from Your own hands the cup, / And to abstain without scorn."[14] The poem challenges what we think of as acceptable or unacceptable love, offering the possibility that all sexual acts and sexual partners could be co-participants in a sacrament given by the gods. Anderson's poem also speaks to abstention as a holy act, with respect and consideration to the one who has offered to share sex. Monogamy, polyamory, asexuality, open relationships, hook-ups—all may be holy relationships with Sex energy. To say yes or no with integrity and respect: this is sexual purity.

From this perspective, we harness and reclaim lust, desire, longing, and arousal as our energy, to share or keep as we will. I may discover deeper sexual satisfaction simply by running life force at home, at work, in worship. If I choose to share sexual energy with others, I do so from a place of joy and power rather than desperation and need. Bringing sexual energy into facets of my life expands my sense of being, pleasure, and joy. Bringing sexual energy to my devotion to the gods enlivens the energetic connection between us.

---

12. Sara Amis, "The World Isn't Disenchanted. It's You," *A Word to the Witch*, 4 September 2015, http://www.patheos.com/blogs/awordtothewitch/2015/09/04/the-world-isnt-disenchanted-its-you.
13. Doreen Valiente, "The Charge of the Goddess," *The Official Doreen Valiente Website*, 5 January 2018, http://www.doreenvaliente.com/Doreen-Valiente-Doreen_Valiente_Poetry-11.php.
14. Victor T. Anderson, "Prayer for Sexual Purification," *Thorns of the Blood Rose* (Cora Anderson, 1970).

The following exercise will help you begin to get a sense of Sex energy:

Start by noticing, as you take in these words, the feeling of being in your body. Notice the weight of your body as it rests against what supports you. Notice the feeling of your breath, and let it slow down. Breathe in, squeezing the kegel muscles behind your bladder and imagining life energy entering through your sex, rising into your body as your belly expands. Exhale, relaxing your kegels and imagining that life force sinking back down through your sex. Breathe into your senses, noticing the feeling of air on your skin and fabric on your body, if any. Notice how sensual this moment is; the cosmos is making love to you simply by offering you sensation and energy. Perhaps your body wants to move slowly to savor the sensations across your skin.

To continue exploring Sex energy, go find a tree or vibrant plant and do this work. Imagine the exchange of energy between you and the plants. Know that as you breathe in, you breathe in life force and connection with all other beings that respire and photosynthesize. The exchange of carbon and oxygen across species is also an exchange of life force, a sexual connection.

When you breathe, fill your body with life force until it feels full. Imagine your animal soul, a sheath of energy extending a few inches around your body, filling with life force and imagine pushing it outward a little further to take in more energy. This part of you is sometimes called Fetch, Sticky One, or Younger Self. Imagine your rational human soul, a spheric aura extending further around your body, filling with life force. This part of you is sometimes called Talker, Shining Body, or Middle Self.

Breathe in the life energy of the plant, and offer back your own life energy. Know that this, too, is Sex. When you feel filled up and joyful, tilt your head back and send some energy on a breath to your God Soul, or Higher Self, which you could envision as a sphere floating slightly over your head. [15]

---

15. This act of feeding God Soul with breath is also known as the "Ha Prayer" in Huna, a New Age metaphysical system claiming to be rooted in Hawaiian spirituality, developed by Max Freedom Long and others. Huna appears to be an appropriative project of white people utilizing indigenous Hawaiian beliefs and practices with dubious to nonexistent consent from indigenous Hawaiian people. The Triple Soul model has antecedents in Huna, though it maps to other esoteric models of the soul. In The Heart of the Initiate, Victor Anderson indicates that his Hawaiian influence comes from his being a kahuna in a previous life, a claim that would not be well received today. I do not think there are any New Age and Pagan practices from the 20th century that did not, at some point, appropriate from indigenous beliefs and practices. I think we must be honest about this, acknowledge a responsibility to represent our practices accurately, and be of service to the people who have been harmed. For an indigenous perspective, see Lisa Kahaleole Hall, " 'Hawaiian at Heart' and Other Fictions," *The Contemporary Pacific*, Volume 17, Number 2, http://hdl.handle.net/10125/13881.

Sex Supported by Pride: Self-Respect

Studying the Iron Pentacle and sacred sexuality in witchcraft has given me a better understanding of the sexual teachings I received in Catholicism. I believe the teachings and practices that many consider repressive and retrograde originated with a recognition of the value of yoking sexuality to Spirit. The teaching became overly narrow and exoteric, however, asserting that sacred sexuality is only to be found within a very specific relationship structure: committed, monogamous, heterosexual marriage. All must therefore themselves fit into this model or deny their sexualities and intimate desires.

So codified, the teachings cease to be life-giving practices that reconnect to Spirit and instead become external standards to which one feels they are "supposed" to adhere and are condemned if one does not. It works for those people who do happen to find their desired sexual partner within that model. For others, having compulsory sex with a person for whom one feels no excitement or attraction offers a deadening vision of relationship with the divine.

When I first turned away from this religion, I thought I had to choose between Sex and Spirit. One of my college friends counted his sexual partners by the hundreds, and his femme energy rankled my conservative upbringing. He showed me a possibility of sex as something joyful and liberating, shared in community and friendship, not simply cordoned off in one kind of relationship. I met gay men who could be friends and have sex, could go to bathhouses together and talk politics, could have sex with each others' partners, and all go have dinner together.[16]

I fell in love with this vision, but soon discovered its shadows. I thought I had to deny my inhibitions and boundaries, willing to give everything to my partners. I felt at war with my shyness, sensitivity, and sexual shame. If I could not be available in any way a partner wanted, I feared that "the right one" would pass me by in favor of someone more free, more wild. My sexual

---

16. This is not an essential or exclusive trait of gay men.

encounters became riskier and exposed me to increasing coercion. My shame, poor self-confidence, and lack of experience negotiating contributed to moments when I crossed others' boundaries in harmful ways. I did not realize until much later that pretending to be without boundary was itself a form of hiding my true Self in all its unfolding complexity.

Owning boundaries, inhibitions, and limitations is a path toward intimacy. Negotiating love between individuals who have unique maps is delicate and challenging, rife with shame and exposure. The art of consent is about engaging each other in exchange, requesting and giving permission for touch and movement. Structured consent practices make this overt and clunky; each movement is specifically requested, evaluated, and decided upon. Learning each others' signs of consent and refusal, building trust, and most of all demonstrating respect for each other's "No" opens up even greater vistas of consent.

One truth I've discovered is that if I ignore my boundaries, they'll still make themselves known. My body will become tense. My voice will grow curt. My words say, "It's fine for you to cancel on dinner," but my tone says, "I am hurt and annoyed. Fuck you." This incongruity erodes trust between partners, revealing as it does the lack of trust within the Self. The anger I swallow today will erupt tomorrow over a slight that has lower stakes. "You always forget to put away the mustard! You never think of how it affects me!"

When I own my "No," my "Yes" becomes more powerful. Once I know my partner will respect my "No," I relax more deeply in connection. My body yields to touch. My heart opens. I go further than I would have expected, and it's okay. And if it's not okay, I know we will stop. My inhibitions, protectiveness, and mistrust do not need to work so hard because they know they have a vote. This state is truly precious in its wonder and rarity.

When I tried to have Sex without Love, I instead became infatuated with every powerful sexual connection and tried, but failed, to flip one-night stands into a long-term relationship. Eventually, through my work with the Sex point, I realized that I was seeking sex out of loneliness and desperation.

My poor boundaries and lack of self-respect led to bad, scary sex and none of the intimacy I craved.[17] I had sex with people I didn't feel excited about. I had sex that felt unpleasant and repugnant because I didn't have the confidence to say no and worried more about their feelings than my own. A few times I had sex in which my boundaries were crossed and I felt coerced, and I struggled even then to validate my feelings.

When we divide Spirit and Matter, that divide runs through Sex. In such a division, you could be a parent and partner, loving, and spiritual; or you can be a sexual being, a slut, a pig, dirty. Rather than destroying Sex, this sundering intensifies the Rusted and Gilded energies around it. That which is made taboo, labeled "dirty" and "degrading," becomes erotic, as the edges of a river give force and direction to the flow of water.

Earthy eros does not need to be separate from emotionally intimate, loving relationships. That erotic energy may simply go dormant, or it may erupt in problematic expressions of conflict and infidelity. We lose enthusiasm and creativity in our work, our home, and our community relationships. This state is the deflated, Rusted point of Impotence. There's no "juice" to bring anything into life. No inspiration. Past failures loom large. We feel creatively and spiritually dead.

The word "Impotence" relates to an inability to maintain an erection, which seems to reduce the scope of the Sex point to penises. Erect male genitalia is not necessary for sex; there are a wide variety of possible acts. This limitation might be a key of exploring this state.

Those in Impotence might experience constraint in spiritual and sexual expression by mental, emotional, or cultural blocks. They might be too focused on a particular kind of sex, a particular state of mind. There is overwhelming pressure to "perform" flawlessly, and the playfulness is gone. In a relationship, a state of Impotence might correspond to fixating on how little

---

17. By "bad" I don't mean "immoral." I mean "disappointing, inadequate, dissatisfying, unskillful." There is a gray area of coercive, bad sex which seems distinct from sexual assault. Rape is about power, control, and non-consensual domination. Bad sex comes from poorly negotiated desires and boundaries.

sex one is having with their partners, to the detriment of ignoring all the other forms of possible connection. Impotence may extend to creative blocks, dark nights of the soul, or being too safe in producing work. When this happens, we need to reconnect with Sex energy. This could be a grand gesture or simply breathing and reconnecting with the senses.

The following exercise offers one way to bring that erotic energy back into relationship with your Higher Self:

Breathe into your center, and as you exhale, imagine roots extending downward from your feet into the earth and branches extending upward from your crown into the sky. Take a breath, noticing the sensations of your body. Take a breath, noticing your emotions and the energetic sheath of energy around your body that is your animal soul. Take a breath, noticing your thoughts and the larger oval that extends around you, your human soul. Breathe upward to the globe of your divinity.

Imagine that everything you notice—where your attention goes—is connected to the center of your forehead by a thread. Breathe, imagining you can pull those threads of awareness into your forehead, forming a ball of consciousness. Let this ball sink through your body, coming to rest in your center. Breathe the edges of this ball to expand and surround you, extending to the edges of that human soul, taking in a soft awareness of your entire being.

Attend to your divine soul, your Higher Self, hovering overhead. This part of the soul is known as the God Soul, Sacred Dove, or Sacred Falcon. What does this part look like to you? Breathe into your imagination the form of your God Soul. Imagine other senses—its texture, its sound.

Now drop your awareness into your sexual organs. Notice the energy therein. Does it feel vibrant, alive? Does it feel numb or cold? Does it feel intense with heat? Notice any judgments that arise in your mind, but try to simply observe and stay with the feelings and energy of your sex. Some associate this energy with serpentine beings. What does this part look like to you? Breathe into your imagination the form of your sex. Imagine other senses—its texture, its sound.

Invite the form of your Sex to rise and the form of your God Soul to descend. They move toward each other in ferocity and lust, each seeking the other. What happens when these energies touch? Stay with this. Be present to the connection and what arises when the two connect. When you are ready, allow these energies to separate again and return to their abodes, above and within. Breathe the energy of this connection to align yourself and feed your God Soul.

SEX FED BY PASSION: EROTIC IMAGINATIONS

In *Mapping the Terrain of the Heart: Passion, Tenderness, and the Capacity to Love*, Stephen Goldbart and David Wallin argue that as adults we form an "inner map" of love and erotic relationships from our histories. Childhood experiences of humiliation, trauma, and powerlessness become erotically charged and manifest in fantasies and fetishes. As adults we may re-create troublesome relationships and circumstances as an unconscious attempt to create a better outcome. At worst, the outcome is the same and feeds a story that begins with "I'll always be..." or "I never will..." Experiencing these as fantasies through conscious, consenting, psychologically safe adult play enables us to contain and transform embedded suffering.

One template for these maps are relationships marked by domination and powerlessness, coalescing in fantasies about power differentials. When contained in the ritual space of the "scene," partners can step into the roles, experience the transformational fantasy, and then step out.

Those roles connect to powerful archetypal energies, shaping our sense of the world and yet are "larger than life." The stern and dominating parent in relationship to the innocent child is one constellation of archetypal relationships. Archetypes are the "deep structures" of the cosmos which become infused with personal content. One person's "Boy" may be quite unlike another's: sometimes anxious and naïve, sometimes canny and seductive. All these fantasies form through lived experience and attach to, for example, the "Boy" or "Girl" archetype, which might itself be a version of the "Divine Child."

Identification with the archetype is dangerous. Projecting the eroticized "Child" energy onto actual human children is violent and abusive. Merging a sense of self with the "Child" archetype would undermine growth toward autonomy, maturity, and responsibility. In my understanding of Jungian psychology, we become conscious of archetypes so that we can separate from them, use the energies consciously without becoming lost. Instead of "being" a "Boy," I connect with that archetype for pleasure, connection, and transformation of childhood wounding around loneliness and desire for validation.

This capacity extends into all kinds of sexual play, and fetishes may meet from very different directions. Some explore the emotionally charged terrain of historical trauma and active oppression through scene enactments of various kinds of domination, degradation, and rebellion. Within a scene, sexual partners may speak to and treat each other in ways that would be deeply hurtful in other contexts. The container of consent allows destructive patterns to have a place of safe venting.

Other kinds of play, less traumatic in origin, may include switching of "roles," gender exploration, teasing, pleasing, and giving or receiving validation. This opens up possibilities to try on new ways of being, to release tension and aggression, or to heal wounds. It is absolutely crucial that participation in these scenes is voluntary and consensual, grounded in mutual respect and an awareness of innate equality.

We're not all mandated to have kinky sex, but many of us have erotic fantasies. The following exercises may help you to reconnect to Passion in your sexuality:

1. Take a moment to slow your breathing down and connect to your sexual energy. Think about the acts, people, and circumstances that you find erotic. If you struggle with this, or want to go deeper, imagine forming the question of "What turns me on?" and dropping it into your core, then watch what arises. You might consider taking a pen or keyboard and writing out what comes to mind, without censoring. Are there particular roles that you imagine yourself in, or does it vary? Are there qualities that you find erotic? Types of relationship?

Do you find any of these qualities in yourself? Are they contrary to who you are in other domains of your life? Is there anyone with whom you can experiment acting out a version of these roles or fantasies in a safe, consensual way? Is there another way to play with these roles in your life?

2. *Find a time and space where you can be alone and explore yourself sexually. Gather toys and other supplies if you like, particularly items that would generate a variety of sensations you can safely try on your body. For this exercise, try not incorporating pornography, drugs, or alcohol. Make love to yourself with your senses and your imagination. Watch yourself if you can. Breathe in sexual energy as you do. Notice when you are caught up in a fantasy and bring presence to your body. Notice what comes up as you do this exercise—shame, longing, joy, pleasure, disgust. Let it all be present in your lovemaking, as best as you can.*

SEX STRENGTHENED BY POWER: CONSENT AND COERCION

The capacity to seduce, arouse, entice, and negotiate consent are powers. As is the capacity to be overcome with desire, to submit to longing, to surrender to another's desires. Power in sex is not something to avoid. Members of the BDSM community have long explored and played with power as a fundamental component of sexual relatedness, and in turn their work highlights how sex is always already embedded in power dynamics.

Pagan communities have ongoing conversations about the relationship between Sex and Power, particularly around protecting vulnerable people from sexual predators, and questioning coercion in relationships with teachers, priests, and priestesses. Dana Corby, who has been studying witchcraft since the 1970s, observes that the practice of Wicca has become less overtly sexual, in part a result of "a pattern, minority but pervasive, of sexual exploitation (mostly of women) by coven leaders (mostly male.)"[18] While she believes most of the sex happening in her communities was consensual, they became aware of abusive individuals. To address this problem, Corby writes, "we tried to eliminate the abuse by desexualizing the Craft, dropping our Tantric practices and making it taboo to even discuss anything of a sexual nature with a student." Corby notes that this had a cost to the students' potential and the vitality of the Craft, losing certain sacred practices and sex-positive cultural norms.

---

18. Dana Corby, "The Rantin' Raven: Wicca Was the Tantra of the West," *Patheos*, 17 October 2015, http://www.patheos.com/blogs/agora/2015/10/the-rantin-raven-wicca-was-the-tantra-of-the-west/

Consensual sex begins with the recognition that all partners have power to exchange willingly, but further recognizes the limits of personal power. No one can force another to become aroused. Neither can we force another to willingly feel enthusiastic desire. We can only learn what draws interest and stokes desire. Power in sex includes the capacity to ask for and receive what we want.

Coercion is "power-over," using whatever strength, leverage, or resources one has to override the choice and agency of one's partners. Coercion may look like withholding love, affection, or access to needed resources. It may be an overt or covert threat, such as an employer able to fire an employee or a wealthier partner able to divorce and humiliate a partner with fewer resources. In spiritual communities powerful leaders, teachers, priestesses, and priests have social capital to marginalize or undermine their students and followers. It's not impossible to have a consenting relationship between people at different levels of power and access. All relationships must wrestle with the issue of power, ideally making space for the greatest freedom and agency of all partners.

Those who have been sexually assaulted or battered by a partner sometimes experience an insistent, forceful kind of "help" in which those around them try to push the victim to take actions that the "helper" believes they need. If the victim does not comply, the "helper" begins to act like a bully as well. We can best support victims by bringing respect to their damaged power and agency, helping them think through their options so that they can make what they see as the best choice.

Even dissociation, that psychic act of "escaping" the body to avoid experiencing the trauma of the moment, is a kind of power and self-protection. At times it is the only protection available for victims during an assault. Unfortunately, it becomes for some survivors a primary, automatic response to threats, which diminishes their capacity to be present in life and cultivate other powers. Mental health and somatic therapies could support these folks in working with the psychic wounds and reclaiming power and agency in their bodies.

Circling The Star

The following working helps with reclaiming life force and sovereignty from coercive experiences. If you decide to do this work, do so in a place where you feel safe at a time when you won't be disturbed. Have a few options of trusted people to call upon if you need support after the working. If you suffer from acute post-traumatic stress and working with trauma memories leads to overwhelming panic, dissociation, substance abuse, or other harmful consequences, then I would recommend establishing a strong personal practice, support network, and relationship with a therapist before engaging in this working.

Gather magical tools, particularly something you consider a symbol of sovereignty. A staff, wand, or blade may represent your personal will or sovereignty in naming, demarcating space, and calling in or banishing energies, just as in history people assigned with responsibilities were given a staff of office. The wand is somewhat more gentle and diplomatic a tool than the blade, which might be useful for its threatening connotations.

Do whatever cleansing or banishing feels appropriate. Alone or with trusted human or spiritual allies, create a sacred space.

Through trance, seek your place of power. If you know the way already, then go there. If not, imagine your feet walking a path toward your place of power. Call up as much sensory information as you can—imagine your feet on the path. What does the path look like? What sounds do you hear? Are there scents?

Find the entrance to your place of power, and go inside. You may wish to explore for a while. Find where you feel strongest and safest within this place of power, and call forth your wand and blade.

Call in a memory of a time when you felt coerced. Recall as much detail as you can. Notice how your body responds to the memory. If you feel overwhelmed, then banish this memory and either complete the working or seek a less stressful memory. Run through the memory once as it happened, then see if you can remember it backwards. Begin at the end of the memory, then remember what happened right before, then right before that, then right before that, until you reach the beginning.

Remember your magical tools. Here, you have all the power. As someone watching this scene unfold, how do you want to help your former self? What tool is appropriate? If you feel stuck, you might ask your former self what support is needed.

You may not change the past, but you can act upon this memory and transform the feelings within it. Take the steps that help you to feel more empowered. Speak the words you wish you could have said. Bind the coercive person. Bring healing to your self.

Let this working continue, and when you are ready, thank yourself for showing up. Ask if there is some practice you need to do that will support your healing. Let go of the memory and return from your place of power. Thank your allies and release the sacred space. Journal, drink water, take a nap, and do whatever self care you need.

SEX EXPRESSING SELF: LONELINESS AND CONNECTION

When I was eleven years old, my family moved to a new town, I started a new school, and two months later my parents separated. For the next few years, my parents seemed distant and preoccupied, and I spent a great deal of time alone in my room. I experienced bullying at school for the first time. There were nights when I laid in bed awake because my loneliness hurt so deeply. It felt like a desperate animal scratching at my heart. In high school, I saw people I would have loved to befriend but felt too afraid and self-doubting. So I simply sat and watched them, feeling more of that pain, no doubt also looking fairly creepy and off-putting.

The lonely part of me is vulnerable, deeply sensitive to isolation and exclusion, experiencing the world as someone unwanted, undesired, unwelcome, and alone. Asking for what I want brings up fears that I will be rejected. When I talk to friends or coworkers, this part of me watches their faces and listens to their voices for signs of irritation and annoyance, signs that I'm not welcome.[19]

At some point I internalized the cultural message that sexual and romantic connection was the antidote to loneliness. If only I met "the one" I

---

19. In *Loneliness: Human Nature and the Need for Social Connection*, John T. Cacioppo speaks of loneliness as "social hunger," an emotional cue that I need to connect. Chronic or protracted loneliness, however, begins to activate the sympathetic nervous system and its "fight or flight" response. Though desperate for connection, mistrust and vigilance are automatic, and it is difficult not to engage protectively at any sign of danger. Unfortunately, this keeps us from the relationships we need.

would be fine, and until then I was condemned. I see this wounding and solution often in lonely people. It might look like spending hours watching romantic movies, falling in love with unavailable people, spending hours seeking casual sex. There is a paradox here: as much as this painful loneliness fixates on connection, it behaves in ways that guarantee disappointment and further isolation. These behaviors elevate romantic and sexual expectations to levels impossible for anyone to meet.

When laden with loneliness and need, Sex becomes too heavy for intimacy. It becomes about proving something, or status, objectifying one's partners by scoring them or tallying them up. We measure sexiness by how much one's body resembles an idealized, objectified form. A form that, thanks to image doctoring, does not exist. Sexiness is about the energy we run, not the way our bodies look.

This state is related to the inflated, Gilded point of Greed. The inner sense of deficiency expresses itself through the pressure to take in more and more sexual energy. The energy of Greed is like a parasitic shell around a lonely person who is starved for intimacy. One person fixates on "getting laid" and looks at their sexual partners as conquests or objects to consume. Another spends hours and hours looking at porn, neglecting important relationships and obligations. Another breaks relationship commitments because they want to have experiences without negotiating with their committed partners.

Greed influences spiritual relationships as well. In my late adolescence and early twenties I found a vision of divine connection in the writings of mystics like Rumi, Hafiz, and Rossetti which seemed the ultimate solution to loneliness. How could I feel alone when I am merged in love with deity? Yet even mystics experience longing, evidenced by their writings. Those moments of ecstatic joining leave a painful emptiness when they inevitably fade.

The antidote to loneliness and Greed is vulnerability. This looks like being emotionally honest about my wants and needs in my relationships, and staying with the messy reality of the moment. I am not guaranteed to get what I want, nor am I required to be all things for another person. We are responsible for our own needs, and yet we need other people to help us meet them. When I allow myself to be vulnerable, my relationships become more genuine and honest, recognizing what we can and cannot offer each other. Instead of imagining one person can do everything for me, I discover a network of relationships that address my needs. Vulnerability opens the way to receive the nourishment I deeply crave. The following exercise can help you with this work:

Spend some time contemplating the following questions. It is useful, if you can, to write down your answers or dictate them to a recorder, as sometimes our answers seem different when we read or hear them versus when we're thinking about them: Do you ever feel lonely? What do you do when you feel lonely? What activities feel like they help distract you from feeling lonely? Do these activities have unwanted consequences?

What activities feel like they help you to be your best self when you're lonely? What people could you call that feel safe, accepting, and responsive? What practices help—prayer, meditation, purification, making offerings and devotions to the gods?

Create a symbol of that part of you that feels lonely, rejected, unwanted, or whatever words feel right. This might be a drawing, a sculpture, or a found object that resonates with this part of you. Carry it with you, or put it in a place of honor. For a week, make a practice of feeding this part of you life force and connection. Notice when you feel connected, at ease, sexy, or confident and send some of this energy to the part of you that feels lonely. Notice when you feel those feelings associated with loneliness, and invite in that energy of connection and sexiness. See how it feels to let these parts of you be connected, instead of trying to get rid of the loneliness.

SEX EXALTED IN LOVE

Asar, Beloved of Kemet, Beloved of the Duat,
Green child of earth and starry heaven,
Gathered and knit back together in Love.
Headless, Your hands are heart-led.
Your heart is Re, eternally giving in golden
Affection, heedless of all affliction.
Upon Your sister's throne, crook and flail
Bring the justice of Ma'at to the people.

When we sit together, our bodies breathe the same air, our energy and expressions respond and create responses in each other. A word, a change in tone, a twitch of the eye from me reaches you and enters your awareness, as do these words. There is an erotic dimension to this connection, even when sexual contact will never occur. Eros is Geb's enticement of Nut: that urge to emerge and merge, the longing for embodiment and experience.

When Spirit and Sex align, Love arises. Physical intimacy, shared with an open heart, helps us to grow more fond, softer, closer. Good sex, cuddling, or even quality time with pets triggers the brain to release the attachment hormone oxytocin, which engenders connection and affection.

When I share sex energy with the gods, with the trees and ocean, I make Love to the world. Pleasure is fuel for Love, though Love extends beyond the hedonic.

A state of connection, sought and feared like Power.
Gravity that binds planets, systems, galaxies.
Pain of heart-opening at the tender, precious,
Fragile and important miracle of being alive.
A lover's eyes mirroring beauty and pain.
Steadiness buffered by raging storms.
Emptiness, a vacuum, a maddening memory
of connection, a longing to be filled, the ache
Of the betrayed heart as yet unhealed.

My experience of Love as Pearl energy is expansive and outward. I give and receive with the same gesture. By loving, I am in Love. The current of Sex runs between the Above and Below through my body, while Love radiates outward horizontally. When I am present to my wholeness, Love radiates and I am in its flow. When I perceive Sex to be blocked or scarce, I withdraw. Unable to fill myself, I seek others to fill me with Love. I feel desperate. I question. I feel restless. I cling to what attention I am offered, even when that attention leaves me feeling degraded and sad.

In the Feri tradition, it is said that the Peacock Lord would become monstrous if not restrained by the hand of Love. The Peacock may expand freely in pride, trusting Love to keep him right-sized. Love greets our limitations, resistances, and inhibitions with gratitude. To grow too large too quickly is a kind of violence to those parts of us that want to stay small. We might approach our resistances, inhibitions, and limitations as the hand of Love helping us to grow at the right speed and remember compassion for those small parts.

For me, Love feels like "turning toward." Therapists and researchers Dr. John and Julie Gottman talk about "bids" for attention in relationships. This is as simple as sitting at the table together and one person reading something funny and going, "Mmm," loudly enough for their partner to hear. That is a bid, an invitation to connect. According to the Gottmans, the other person could respond by turning toward, turning away, or turning against. A person who turns toward could respond with some warm version of, "Mm?" or "What's that?" A person who turns away might simply ignore the noise or get up and go to the kitchen for more water. A person who turns against might become irritated at the interruption, with a harsher "What do you want?" or "I'm trying to read here."[20]

When I first watched the videos illustrating these behaviors, I cringed. I was terrible at turning toward. I experienced other people's bids for attention as irritating and intrusive. This came from a deeply ingrained personality pattern of withdrawal and guardedness about my inner life. Turning toward did not always feel safe—sometimes I was ridiculed or bullied by other kids, sometimes I felt fearful of my father's anger or guarded against my mother's needs for emotional support. I buried and twisted my own need for attention such that I came to believe that the only way to be worthy of positive attention was to give no outward sign of desiring it. When others were open and honest about their desires for attention, I was judgmental about it. I also envied it.

Turning toward feels like a simple but rich practice. Instead of writing a list of shoulds, I begin by noticing the direction of my energy in relationship to what is in my world. Bids for attention show up in all of our relationships. A spirit of place might bring my attention to trash on the ground, and turning toward could be stopping to pick it up. When I notice a particular god is on my mind, or symbols of the god show up unexpectedly, I see that as a bid for attention. When I notice myself reciting prayers by rote, I turn toward by taking a breath and returning to the practice with more vigor. When my

20. John Gottman, *The Relationship Cure* (New York: Harmony, 2001).

body signals me with hunger and tiredness, I turn toward by slowing down, napping, or preparing food. When I notice a perpetual problem in community that irritates me, I turn toward by attempting to address the issue.

Turning toward is a practice of immanent religion. If the world and everything in it is a part of the body of God Hirself, then its "mundanities" matter and are worthy of care and attention. Periods of solitude and retreat need not be about disconnection, rather turning toward the Inner Self for its spiritual work. This energetic rhythm of connection, turning in and turning out, keeps us in flow with God Hirself.

Practicing love brings us more deeply into the heart of life. If you keep going, you may turn toward things that terrify you, disgust you, make you uncomfortable, and find what is worthy dwelling within. You may find this world is not a vale of horrors, though horror is within it. You may find yourself more at home wherever you go.

Asar, better known by his Greek name Osiris, is a Kemetic sacral ruler who gazes upon his kingdom with loving concern and attention. He has known the rule of sun and dark, the living and the dead. He endures dismemberment by his brother Set and is re-membered by the loving efforts of his wife Auset (or Isis, great of magic and goddess who represents the throne of Egypt), lover Nebt-Het (or Nepthys, lady of the temple house and goddess of nourishment and sacrifice), and child Anpu (or Anubis, jackal-headed psychopomp and priest of funerary rites). Asar needed others, as we need others.

Pain, anger, mistrust, and sorrow are a hard soil in which to plant Love. Yet a Love that cannot endure these feelings will not last. It is like the tree that has never grown hardy through enduring strong winds; easily uprooted by the first hard gust. Suffering and disappointment initiate us into the darker mysteries of Love.

Beauty sapped of vitality by cancer.
Joyful babies who will suffer.
Despair at watching your beloved in pain.
Leaving a lover to save your wild heart.

These mysteries are "dark" because they are deeper, richer soil. They ground Love into something more somber and resilient. Love calls us to bind ourselves to the fate of something larger than the ego. Commitment carries Love through hurt, hardship, and change. The seventh house of Western astrology governs marriage and open enemies, and sometimes those relationships are hard to tell apart.

Commitment that has become solely pain and hardship becomes depleting and void of joy. Sex energy tends the dying body as much as the living one. In so many myths passed to us from our ancestors, lovers risked sanity and life by descending into the underworld to find and remember their deceased loves, as Auset did when she brought Asar's parts back together for one last moment of intimacy.

According to Morpheus Ravenna, Celtic peoples believed that the loss or disabling of a limb meant that it now lived in the realms of the dead, and thus had access to spiritual power.[21] A blind eye sees the spirit realms. When we lose our loved ones through death or ruptures in relationship, might those parts of us that loved follow them into the realms of the dead? Could grief be a portal to the underworld? Is Grief the midnight name of Love?

By the time we're in our early adulthood we've written much of the inner "map" of Love through failures of attachment, betrayals, moments of beautiful connection and joy, and the cultural stories imprinted upon us through media. We are told in so many ways how Love is supposed to look, how often and inevitably hearts are broken, how we need to be strong and protect ourselves from dangerous manipulators but also vulnerable enough to receive love. We hear stories about "the one" and "the love of my life" and some unlucky folks spend years looking for it and others spend years fearing they've already had and lost it. We resent our parents for failures and mistakes. We idolize our parents and want their approval. We want our parents to heal wounds they made and wounds they didn't know they made. We want our lovers to heal the wounds our parents and ex-lovers made. We want our friends to heal the wounds our lovers make.

21. This was communicated in a workshop Morpheus Ravenna led at Mythic Worlds in 2016.

When my husband asked me to marry him, I had all these ideas about what marriage was supposed to be, few of which prepared me for what actual marriage has been. Trying to make my marriage match those "supposed to be" stories left me disappointed and resentful, whereas accepting our relationship as it is has made me happier and freer.

These "supposed to's" included: partners are never supposed to confront each other, only support; partners should always want to have sex with each other and should do so consistently, regularly, and exclusively; partners' interests should be completely aligned; partners should like each others' friends; partners should spend most of their free time together; partners should always make each other feel better about themselves.

None of these expectations are "wrong," but they come from outside the relationship rather than emerging from the genuine needs and wants of the people in the relationship. When I do not tolerate confrontation and difficult feedback, my husband has no space to communicate what's not working for him. If my husband and I have to always spend our time together, we do not have room to grow as people and develop unique interests. If I'm at my worst and treating my husband like shit, he might not be in the mood to make me feel better about myself. Indeed, "make me feel better about myself" is a huge task to assign to another person.

Unstated expectations foment resentment, and harbored resentment kills Love. In relationship, all we see are the behaviors of other people; not their motivations, thoughts, feelings, or inner struggles. When I have unexamined expectations, my mind fills in that missing information with a story in which I'm the victim. When I share those expectations, however, we have a chance for understanding and better agreements. If the other person disrespects the conscious agreement, we have definite grounds for complaint.

Intimate love relationships seem to be about making each partner whole, but not in the way we're told by romantic propaganda. Another person does not complete us by compensating for our lack. Instead, the committed relationship itself becomes a mirror by which we see what in us needs healing and balancing.

The desire to be *completed* points to imbalance in the personality; one facet is overvalued and another is seemingly nonexistent. At first we see in our partners what we feel is lacking. Once the initial rush of passion wears off, however, that difference becomes grating. This longing and irritation both signify that we are projecting; what we see in our partners is a shadow part of ourselves to name and claim.

In all realms, even the intimate ones, the Divine Twins dance. The Twins are the children and lovers of God Hirself, divine opposition born from Hir creative energies: thesis and antithesis, light and dark. If I and my partner lean on each other, one of us will fall if the other needs to step away. If we lean away from each other, straining to keep a hold on the relationship, again one of us will fall if the other shifts. When we learn to stand on our own and stay connected, we can step away and return, join hands or simply be in each other's presence. This shifts the relationship away from a painful war over needs towards something more autonomous and more intimate.

My heart wants to be protected from hurt. My ego wants to be defended against invalidation. Part of me wants to personalize others' disagreements with me, their broad criticisms. When I allow myself to be entangled in conflict, my intention and will become derailed. More of my energy is spent defending and protecting rather than creating.

Jesus Christ guided his followers to love one's enemies and pray for those who would persecute them. Buddhists practice lovingkindness meditation by beginning with what is easiest to love and moving toward what is most challenging. Witchcraft, in contrast, teaches that anger is an acceptable emotion, and occasionally we must get our hands dirty in the service of what we Love. The witch knows the rage of the scorned earth, the love of the nettle and the protective mother whose cubs are in danger. To shape the world, we must stand for something. Without that, we become whelmed in the larger forces that unconsciously drive the world. Standing for what we value makes us conscious actors, and brings us up against that which opposes and resists our values. I must know what I am for to manifest a better world.

When conflict invites me to choose a "side," however, I become tempted to fall into sectarian lures: that one "side" is right or good and the other is wrong or bad. Then the further lures, that our good side is unimpeachable, righteous, above critique, and the other bad side is without redeeming value, has nothing to offer. Then we risk the danger of justifying everything shitty our side does and says and excoriating everything the other side does and says. We are at risk of dismissing the other "side's" genuine needs and concerns. We are at risk of getting caught in minor squabbles instead of investing in the world we desire. The Divine Twins are made to hate each other rather than reflect each other's wholeness.

As the witch finds Love in darkness and horror, I strive to connect in Love to those things and people that offend parts of me. This led me to become a therapist and practice offering love to those parts of me and other people who feel unworthy of it. Parts of me are still very much mired in conditional love, disgust, aversion, and prejudice. I agonized about this in my graduate internship with a client that I found deeply unlikeable. I wondered how I could be of help to him. One of my classmates suggested that if I couldn't be loving, I could at least be be real. I could reflect honestly what I was seeing and hearing, not punishing him with abandonment and harshness but also not coddling him by avoiding honesty. This became a touchstone practice for me, a way of engaging in the practice of Love even when my heart feels at its limits.

Being real is itself a form of connection and Love, eschewing false faces of niceness. Love may be direct and fearsome, it may cut through the bullshit and save us all time and stress. I see this kind of Love in long-term social workers who are intimately familiar with the system and its disappointments and have lost enough illusions that they accept people as they are. They continue to show up to the work at hand, stripped of idealism and a certain amount of sentimentality, attending to the needs and possibilities of the moment. I suspect this is similar to the state of being Reclaiming witch Donald Engstrom speaks of as the "Cold Heart of Compassion."

Love that requires extraordinary virtue is a conditional experience, one that will wither with time. Love would not have us be so fragile. Love would take away every condition we place upon existence, would challenge every expectation, leaving behind only the purest capacity for acceptance and presence in the heart. True intimacy is presence with everything that occurs. Every condition and expectation is another illusion veiling the potential Love.

To be in the flow of Love is to be in a state of calling and giving out, being filled and pouring out, a dynamic state. This returns us to the ladder of Spirit, ascending, descending, and centering. Spirit is the element that changes expression as soon as it is named. Spirit, Sex, and Love are evolutionary forces. There is no stasis here, no winner or loser, only the longings of our soft bodies and the knowledge of our hearts.

Air, Self, Knowledge: Solve et Coagula

Before the beginning, there was a great expanse, the waters of Nun. When the creator god set about shaping the worlds from the waters, nothingness, darkness, and infinity, a drop of his creative seed fell into the waters of Nun. On the first day Ra crossed the sky and shone upon the waters, the bud of a blue lotus emerged from the primordial ocean and opened to drink in life force. Within that bud was Nefertum, beautiful one, who looked upon the world with joy. Realizing that he was alone, however, broke his heart open with sorrow, and he wept. Each tear fell upon the petals of the lotus and dripped upon the new, empty land. From the mixture of these tears and the dry soil, humanity was born.

Self is our home and source. It is a process, adapting to the environment and generating new expressions. It is also a result, a momentary image of all the experiences we have accrued in life. Western occultism does not require the denial of Self. Indeed, many forms of occultism enlarge the Self until it encompasses the world. A change within the Self causes real and profound change in the world, as changes in the world affect the Self, but only when we allow the exchange of within and without.

The center of stillness within the Self corresponds to the body's physical center of gravity. The body's orientation, balance, and adaptation to changing circumstances depend upon the center of gravity. When I walk up a hill, my body naturally curves forward so that my center of gravity does not pull me backwards, and vice versa when walking downhill. When I fall off-balance, my physical adjustments move my center of gravity back to a stable position. Cultivating the center of stillness and giving it more density makes it more like an inner Sun: its gravity helps our many parts move in a spacious, polyrhythmic system.

AIR AND SELF

Like Air, Self is diffuse yet occupies space, taking the form of that which contains it. We observe the Self through its expressions—our role in society, community, family, and relationship. To confuse these expressions for the Self, however, separates us from purpose and depth. Our energy is spent endlessly appeasing others. The ever-creative source of Self remains within, inviting attention through whispers of sensation, thought, and feeling.

Acceptance and Commitment Therapy (ACT), a psychotherapeutic approach informed by behavioral, Existentialist, and Buddhist psychologies, uses the phrase "self-as-content" to describe a psychologically rigid state of being. In this state, "I am" is identified with the content of my experience: "I am stupid." "I am sad." "I am sick." "I am depressed." In this state, we experience suffering because the inner problem eclipses our desires.

With self-as-content, we tend to fixate on external solutions to those perceived internal problems. If my story is, "I am a piece of shit," then I must either concede to that or constantly make effort to look like a person who is not a piece of shit. Yet by succumbing or wrestling with the thought, I validate it. "I have to keep working late so I don't mess up and everyone won't see that I'm a piece of shit."

ACT contrasts this with the more flexible "self-as-context." In this view, "I am" the space in which my thoughts, feelings, and bodily sensations occur. With the observing part of self, "I am" able to bear witness to experience and remain conscious. I notice that when I have conflict with friends, the thought "I am a piece of shit" comes up and leads me to want to withdraw. I notice feelings with that thought, and how it reminds me of things that happened in childhood. These thoughts and feelings are not problems to solve but simply information that helps the "I am" to make better choices. All of my parts have room to exist and be in relationship.

Self-as-context encompasses the solar system, whereas self-as-content focuses on one or two objects within it. Space allows each of our parts, our planets, to move in the rhythm and orbit that suits them. Without space, every object would be dissolved in the Sun.

The following meditation moves awareness from self-as-content to self-as-context. You may wish to have a friend read it to you, or to record yourself leading it and then use the recording to anchor your experience. Read at a slow, even pace, and allow long pauses between each sentence.

Find a place where you can sit undisturbed, preferably on something that will support your posture. Lengthen your spine, the top of your head stretching upward and allowing the rest of your body to straighten beneath it. Slow your breathing down. Breathe through your nose if you can, and let your awareness rest on the feeling of the air moving in and out of your body.

Notice what is happening in your mind. Notice thoughts, commenting on the past or the future, or commenting on what is happening right now. Watch these thoughts arise and pass away as though they are actors on a stage and your awareness sits in the audience. When you notice yourself caught in a thought—going from one thought to the next, analyzing, telling a story, "figuring something out"—call your awareness back to this witnessing, anchored by breath. Spend a few minutes with this.

Let your awareness drop into your heart. Notice any emotions that are present. See if you can watch these feelings, again like actors on a stage, with your awareness in the audience. Spend a few minutes with this. If you find yourself caught in an emotion or thought, let your breath bring you back to witnessing.

Let your awareness sink into your belly and expand into your body. Notice what physical sensations are present. Watch these sensations, letting them be without trying to make adjustments or suppress them. Continue bringing your awareness to breath if you find yourself caught in a sensation, thought, or feeling.

Now soften your awareness and try to observe your whole self: thoughts... sensations... emotions... Let your awareness rest in the center of yourself, in the still center in your body, simply being present to what is happening within you.

Notice the space between your thoughts and sensations. Notice how much space there is between your thoughts and the pressure of the floor beneath you. Notice how much space there is between the feeling of air on the skin of your face and the still place within. Breathe into this space, letting it open and relax. Everything in you can be there, where it is, but your attention dwells on the space between. If you are caught up in a thought or feeling, breathe your awareness back to the still center and open from there.

Stay with this open, spacious experience of Self. Notice what it is like to be in this state. Ask your still center if there is a word, image, or gesture that could be your key back to this expanded state of being. When you are ready, thank yourself and all your parts for being present, and bring your awareness back to your environment.

SELF REVEALED IN POWER: IDENTITY

Self clothes itself with identity. To begin naming your identities, finish the statement: "I am a/n ..." Today I am a son, brother, husband, therapist, and mentor. Some of these identities feel deeply meaningful, while others were given to me without much consideration. Identities may come from experiences of the Self, like "survivor." Others are names for systems of belief that resonate—like "Stoic," "Socialist," or "Pagan." Identity makes possible communication and analysis of the Self, by naming.

The very necessity and act of communication establishes identity as relational. A word like "son" implies that I have a person who would identify as my parent. To identify as a "Stoic" is to put one's self in community with others who ascribe to Stoicism, or have a stoic personality.

This facet of relationship (community and identity) is also a site of deep wounding. If I say I am this kind of person and everyone around me denies it, undermines it, mocks it, marginalizes it, rejects it, or simply ignores it, then that part of me suffers and putrefies. Personal work and sheer willpower might be enough to maintain its health, but that draws energy that could be better spent. Toni Morrisson speaks to this with regard to racism:

> The function, the very serious function of racism is distraction. It keeps you from doing your work. It keeps you explaining, over and over again, your reason for being. Somebody says you have no language and you spend twenty years proving that you do. Somebody says your head isn't shaped properly so you have scientists working on the fact that it is. Somebody says you have no art, so you dredge that up. Somebody says you have no kingdoms, so you dredge that up. None of this is necessary. There will always be one more thing.[22]

Those whose identities are not honored by the majority culture experience an onslaught of hostility on a daily basis, unrecognized by those who fit more easily. When the world around you generally agrees with your worldview, it is hard to recognize the alienation and the shame it heaps upon those with a different view. The attack on identity fosters stress, anxiety, defensiveness, and hostility.

Though I was identified as a male at birth and feel that identity mostly fits, I've experienced attacks in which others questioned whether I am "a man" because I did not behave or look like what they thought "a man" should. My identity suffered injury, and now I feel a defensiveness and anxiety when I hear a particular phrase, a particular tone, or someone insults me in a way that resembles earlier insults. Intellectually, I understand that no one can tell me what "being a man" truly is, especially as what makes a man changes over time. I may find myself, however, manipulated into doing something I don't want to do simply because someone implied I'm "not a man" if I don't do it.

There are ways my maleness is not attacked as a transgender man's might be. Most people refer to me by male pronouns without my asking. I use the men's bathroom without fear. Peers and authorities recognize and acknowledge my maleness without any effort on my part. When I apply for jobs, I don't have to explain why the person I was five years ago had a

---

22. Toni Morrison, "Transcript: Toni Morrison at Portland State, 1975," 7 July 2014, https://mackenzian.com/blog/2014/07/07/transcript-morrison-1975/.

different name and gender. Security agents at the airport do not question why my ID and my gender presentation do not seem to line up.

As social animals we have, I believe, an instinctive part of us that craves belonging. We know that babies thrive when they experience touch and warmth from their caregivers.[23] We know that solitary confinement increases the risk of mental illness in prisoners.[24] Some parts of us experience threats of exile and abandonment as threats to well-being and survival. Bullying, refusal to use the correct name or pronouns, or any experience of being made to feel unwelcome is a threat to this belonging-needing part of self.

It's not simply a minor irritation. We feel stress when we suffer the quiet contempt of someone who does not consider us worth treating with basic respect. Imagine feeling that stress multiple times a day, sometimes when least expected, by friends or family or coworkers, or by strangers.

As with many psychic wounds, when we get a taste of exile or abandonment, we develop strategies to avoid re-experiencing this pain. The strategies become problematic to ourselves and communities when we:

- Become deeply invested in identity, trying to be "the best [x] I can" so no one can judge or exclude us. This may get us some mileage, but the trauma is magnified when we lose that identity. Someone who has spent years being "a good son" suddenly becomes utterly lost when his parents die. This strategy is also incredibly challenging in a society in which we may hold multiple identities with widely varying norms and expectations.
- Minimize the need for community and connection altogether, disavowing any identity that requires others' validation. A less intense version of this looks like cultivating a guarded distance, so one is a member of the community but rigidly holds oneself as an edge-walker, critic, or observer—all necessary roles, but ideally ones we step in and out of over time.

---

23. Victoria Costello, "Five Ways to Create a Secure Attachment with Your Baby, Without Sharing Your Bed," *PsychCentral*, https://psychcentral.com/lib/five-ways-to-create-a-secure-attachment-with-your-baby-without-sharing-your-bed/.
24. George Dvorsky, "Why Solitary Confinement Is The Worst Kind Of Psychological Torture," *Gizmodo*, 1 July 2014, https://io9.gizmodo.com/why-solitary-confinement-is-the-worst-kind-of-psycholog-1598543595.

- Develop rigid expectations of what someone with [x] identity should look like or act like, what values they should hold, what politics they should espouse—all of which centralizes one's own values, attitudes, and behaviors. Doing so, we limit growth and development.
- Express defensive outrage or excessive victimization at signs of criticism or accountability from others within the community.
- Police community boundaries—enacting rigid identity norms by marginalizing anyone who doesn't fit through social control strategies such as gossiping, bullying, excluding from social events or positions of influence, or simply denouncing the person as "not a true [x]." Thus we become hostile to the natural and productive diversity within our communities.

These dynamics of rigidity, perfectionism, intolerance for difference, and avoidance of open-hearted confrontation and compromise are toxic to any community. I believe these dynamics intensify in communities of people who themselves grew up feeling alien or rejected. Once we find a place where we feel accepted, welcome, and seen, that taste of joy makes us initially zealous in our devotion, and resolved never to lose that belonging. Unhealed, these underlying identity injuries direct our actions. We end up marginalizing others in our communities, projecting our own trauma, and making it a social norm.

Developing other facets of Self helps to heal and relax these dynamics. When I validate my identity and remember it isn't "me," I feel less vulnerable when someone attacks it. Becoming aware of what the identity means to me—what I think defines the identity based on my lived experience—gives me inner authority. If one community is taking up too much time and attention, it's worthwhile to engage in other interests, connect with trusted family, or engage with other friends. When I step out for a moment I feel more perspective on what's going on, take it less personally, and re-engage with more openness and appreciation. I remember that I am more than this identity, and also recognize that every community has issues.

Circling The Star

One exercise often used to teach Self in the Iron Pentacle is a process of shedding layers of identity until reaching our core.[25] A similar exercise is the Vedic practice known as "Neti Neti" (or "Not this, Not that") in which one asks one's Self, "Who am I?" and waits for the answer, then refutes the answer. For example, "Who am I?" "I am a man." "No, that is a gender role assigned to me. Who is the I that is gendered male?" This practice continues until arriving at the answer that feels correct, which I have experienced as a deep sense of knowing, a sense of "Yes, this is it." The answer that was correct ten years ago may not be the answer that is correct today.

The following exercise provides an opportunity to reflect on your identities and what parts of you get included and excluded by each:

What identities do you claim? Make a list of them. Write out as many as you can think of, especially the silly ones, private ones, or scary-exciting ones. Look at your list, and find one that feels the most charged with feeling and energy.

Take a blank sheet of paper, and write that identity in the center. Draw three concentric circles around it. In the innermost circle, write words or phrases describing the identity as you'd like it to be, your hopes and dreams, your most valued qualities of these identities. In the middle circle, write the words or phrases that you think most people who share your identity would use to describe it. In the outer circle, write the words or phrases that you think most people who are outside of your community would use to describe your identity. In the margins outside the outermost circle, write any words or phrases that seem outside of your identity, outside of what you or your community associate with it.

Look at these marginal words and notice if any feel particularly intriguing or exciting. Circle that, and breathe the energy of this word into your aura. Do some creative work envisioning how that word or phrase could be included in this identity: freewriting, make a collage, write a poem, dance the energy, whatever feels right. Make a commitment to yourself to attend to this energy for the next week, looking for opportunities to include it in your daily life or interactions within the community.

---

25. A version of it is written in T. Thorn Coyle's *Evolutionary Witchcraft*.

Self Grounded by Pride: Paradoxical Integrity

Beginning a dedicated meditation practice showed me how much my inner solar system was in chaos and conflict. I would try to follow the simple direction of "notice your breathing" and immediately parts of my brain would want to do other things. On a deeper level, I began to notice how what I said I wanted didn't line up with the way I was acting. Parts of me were in conflict.

In the West, we have trouble thinking of ourselves "containing multitudes," as Whitman wrote. The ego works to maintain the impression that we have a unitary perspective, a core consistent experience, until we make effort to recognize how many contradictions and conflicting desires we have. I think of the ego as the empty command chair. Whomever sits upon the chair commands the ship. The ship cannot sense whether Commander Rational or First Lieutenant Asshole is giving the orders, it simply responds and thinks of all as "me."

During the recession of 2008, when I was unemployed, I kept doing job manifestation magic that would fail. There were many reasons for this, such as my failure to recognize the energetic tidal wave of the economy that was at odds with my stated desire. Internally, I started to recognize that parts of me resisted the magic because they hated my previous job. I'd been thinking about changing careers for a while, but I'd hesitated because I was hooked on the illusion of stability from my corporate job. Eventually I decided that I had nothing to lose, so I decided to go back to school.

During my program, I had another problem. I'd decided to do a practicum, which was not required but would make me more employable in the future. The problem was, I'd spent an entire quarter of practicum only accruing four service hours when I needed thirty. I repeatedly asked for help getting more service hours but was told to sit tight. By the second quarter I worried that I would have to go into yet another quarter, push back my plans to graduate, and go into deeper debt. I wondered whether to abandon the practicum altogether, but every time I resolved to leave I would burst into tears. There was much I loved about the practicum work, as little as there was.

My heart resisted the choice that my mind thought most rational, so I made a deal with myself: I would finish the second quarter, get what I could from the experience, and move on whether I'd finished the hours or not. After making this choice, I met with a woman who had been abruptly reassigned as my academic advisor, who saw my problem and took immediate action to get me another practicum site. Though it took some hustling, I was able to get all the hours I needed on time.

From this I learned much about inner conflict. The mind is excellent at analysis, thinking through possibilities, identifying potential obstacles, and planning. The mind "processes" the information available. When that process disconnects from conditions on the ground, the mind stops receiving new information and instead loops through old information in paralyzing and misleading ways. Emotions and felt senses in the body offer new information for the mind to process. A strange, nagging discomfort points toward the subtle indicators that this path is not right for me, or this person not trustworthy.

The heart is excellent at depth, meaning, and connection but without the mind it may draw us toward actions that are not in alignment with reason, prudence, and ethical judgment. My feelings might come from old woundings or other people's emotions. Instincts keep me safe but may stymie me from pursuing the life that I want.

Training our parts to cooperate helps us discern which patterns of thought, feeling, and behavior are toxic, and sink deeper to learn what purpose those patterns serve. I believe all human behavior is purposeful, though often that purpose is unconscious and paradoxical. An inward sense of constant terror and hypervigilance expresses itself outwardly as hostility. An outward expression of critical parenting relates to an inward desire to protect one's child.

When the unconscious purpose and conscious desire conflict, we need to bring them into conversation. Turning the paradox inside-out can shift an unworkable pattern into a workable one. The hostile man, for example, needs to find internal safety so he can set softer and more effective boundaries. The critical parent might need to practice allowing their child to experiment on their own, so the child can develop confidence.

Judgments about parts being "good" or "bad" do not come from the God Soul, which offers endless love, compassion, and acceptance. These judgments come when we squeeze our entire Self into a narrow part of the personality. When pleasing others is the most important quality, it feels "wrong" to do something for one's self. Also, too much investment in ambition leaves one feeling "lazy" when they want to take a break. Yet these "bad" urges have something important to offer, something that brings resilience and more integrity to the Self.

Rusted, deflated energy of Self is called Deprecation, an example of self-defeating paradoxical behavior. A person in Deprecation acts out constant self-effacement, self-negation, and self-mockery. It almost looks like they take pride in their worthlessness. This shows up often in people who experienced extensive bullying and invalidation as children, who decided, "It's better if I make the joke before someone else does." In less extreme versions, people apologize or put themselves down when stepping forward: "No one's going to care about this, but..." "I'm not as smart as you all, but..."

Deprecation is a public self-abasement. Others feel an urge to reassure or compliment the person, thinking they simply need an ego boost, only to find the person in Deprecation arguing back that yes, they really are that bad. Deprecation is false humility, denying innate strengths, gifts, wants, and needs while simultaneously broadcasting them. Deprecation inevitably leads to resentment, the feeling that arises when we repeatedly set aside our wants and needs. Deprecation has many faces, but all seem to prevent the person from connecting to the creative source of the Self.

One antidote to Deprecation is self-respect. This is the loving and honest acknowledgment of myself as I am today in all my parts. With self-respect I practice not insulting myself, not minimizing my thoughts and gifts, but instead offering them as they are and waiting to see how others respond.

The following exercise may support you in cultivating a better listening relationship with the parts of you that feel hard to honor.

Think about a quality you have that you dislike, or struggle with, or outright hate. You might look at patterns of thought, feeling, or behavior, both internally or in your relationships with others. Think about what you often run up against, or where your self-deprecating language often shows up, especially statements like: "I hate how I..." "I never..." "I always..." Alternately, pick a quality that really annoys you about others and try the exercise as though it were true of you.

Write a paragraph or draw a picture to represent the pattern. Identify what beliefs you have about why this pattern came to be, or what purpose it serves.

Then stand up and shake off the process so far. Invoke the energy of this pattern into your body, and align it with your God Soul. Sit down and free-write in response to the following questions, whatever answers come to mind, but write from the "I" perspective of this energy. Let it move through you, writing whatever words come to mind without censorship or worrying about accuracy. Use whatever divination materials you are best acquainted with to ask for more insight into the following questions.

What need is this pattern trying to meet?

What is the hidden strength?

What does this tendency point toward?

When you feel finished, shake off this energy. Take some time away. Later, reread these answers and the writing you did before. Ask this part of you, "How can we work in greater integrity?" Do some free-writing in response to this question. See if you can come up with a simple practice that will help you to remember your intention to have a different relationship with this part of Self.

SELF EMERGING THROUGH PASSION: CENTER AND CIRCUMFERENCE

We learn who we are through what others reflect to us. During her 2010 TED Talk, Brené Brown defines empathy as the capacity to *feel with* another person: "In order to connect with you, I have to connect with something in myself that knows that feeling."[26] Empathy has a mutuality as opposed to

---

26. Brené Brown, "The Power of Vulnerability," June 2010, https://www.ted.com/talks/brene_brown_on_vulnerability.

sympathy, which Brown states comes from a position of superiority. There is no shared feeling. The sympathetic person peers down at the hurting person safely from their perch of emotional distance.

In her own 2010 TED Talk, Roshi Joan Halifax provides an important expansion with the concept of compassion, which she asserts has the following components: the capacity to "see clearly into the nature of suffering," the aspiration "to transform suffering," and the essential component "that we cannot be attached to outcome."[27]

Pulling it all together: compassion is empathy plus boundaries, minus attachment. To have empathy, I must be able to see in myself the reflection of your feelings, and feel with you. To have compassion, I must be able to recognize that these are your feelings, and support you in finding the transformation of your suffering. Compassion opens the doors of connection and authentic support.

The rush to fix or dismiss others' problems comes from discomfort with facets of Self. If your problem brought up feelings in me that I label as "bad" or unwanted, then I would pull back from connection. I would want to stop you from "feeling bad" (or at the very least talking about it!) so that I don't have to "feel bad." Dividing up these experiences into good or bad, wanted or unwanted, impedes the flow of life energy and connection. Emotional defenses in one elicit emotional defenses in the other.

When a person offers me advice from a place of sympathy or fixing, even if it is sound, I find it hard to receive. I sense they don't get me and I don't trust them. I might outwardly concede, but I do not take in the advice and make it my own. Attempts to follow the advice without this ownership look half-hearted. I expect to fail so I can go back to the person and say, "See? This didn't work. Now you have to listen to me." When I feel heard and understood, when I sense this person respects my struggle and ambivalence and is coming to me as a fellow human being, then my defenses soften and I become more open to their advice.

27. Joan Halifax, "Compassion and the True Meaning of Empathy," December 2010, https://www.ted.com/talks/joan_halifax.

Humans are wired to emotionally influence each other. The mind imagines, and the body responds. This extends to seeing emotions in the faces, vocal inflections, and body postures of another person.[28] To see another's contempt is to feel its effects upon you. To see sadness is to feel sadness. To be surrounded by a crowd of cheering sports fans is to feel swept up in the excitement.

Hostility in marital conflict has a significant detrimental effect on the immune system, according to Daniel Goleman.[29] Being on the receiving end of a contemptuous statement, eye roll, or facial expression is enough to stress and weaken the immune response. The difference between contempt and anger is similar to that of sympathy versus empathy. Contempt comes from a position of superiority and dominance. It's the position of, "You're an idiot," or "That's so stupid." Goleman notes that couples who learn to fight fair, which is more of a position of equality and humility, decrease the negative health effects of conflict.

Accepting this susceptibility as truth challenges the idea that it is possible to be emotionally unaffected by others. The "strong" person who seems unphased or to "give no fucks" is valorized as an ideal to which we should aspire. This is at great cost to the "strong" person themselves, who feel the pressure to maintain this strength even in moments when they desperately need to collapse, to allow themselves to feel and to hurt. We cannot maintain a constant level of euphoria, enthusiasm, determination, happiness, or whatever "positive" emotion we celebrate.

What I find more workable than machismo is something teacher T. Thorn Coyle writes: "Our work is not to remain completely calm and smooth at all times. Our work is to be able to return to our center as quickly as possible in the midst of upheaval."[30] In our center of Self is a deep well of stillness and resilience. A daily practice of centering and sitting in medita-

---

28..Elaine Hatfield, John Cacioppo, and Richard Rapson, *Emotional Contagion* (Cambridge: Cambridge University Press 1994).
29. Daniel Goleman, "New Light on How Stress Erodes Health." *New York Times*, 15 December 1992, http://www.nytimes.com/1992/12/15/science/new-light-on-how-stress-erodes-health.html.
30. T. Thorn Coyle, *Kissing the Limitless: Deep Magic and the Work of Transforming Yourself and the World* (San Francisco: Weiser 2009)..

tion strengthens that center. When I know my center, I sense my boundaries. Working with center and circumference aids in differentiating whether feelings are mine or another's.

The following practice helps with connecting to center and circumference. Try doing the full process once a day for a month.

Slow your breathing down. Let your shoulders remain still as you breathe in, filling your belly, and then breathe out completely. Notice what is present right now: thoughts... feelings... sensations in the body.

Notice your environment... any sounds... the temperature... the feeling of air on your skin... the ground beneath you... Notice the relationship between your thoughts, feelings, and body and what is happening in the environment.

Sense your center. For many, it is between your navel and your pelvis. If it feels significantly higher, see if you can allow it to drop a little. Sense or imagine the stillness within it. Send a breath into this stillness and imagine your center becoming more dense, more sturdy. Continue breathing into this still center for five breaths. Now sense or imagine the edges of your aura, extending out from your body in the shape of an egg or sphere. What do these edges feel like today?

Inhale into your still center, and exhale, sending energy out to the edges of your aura. With every inhalation, center yourself, and with every exhalation, let your aura become centered around this stillness. Send energy to any part of your aura that needs cleansing or healing.

Inhale again into your still center, and breathe out forcefully, expelling anything that is not yours from your energy bodies. Breathe earth energy through your feet into your center, and breathe out to strengthen your edges. Does your circumference need to be more solid, to better filter others' energy? Does your circumference need to be more porous, to allow more effective empathy and communication? Send whatever energy that is needed out from your still center.

Once you feel you understand the process energetically, you may simplify the practice and draw upon it when you feel or encounter intense emotions. When I worked customer service, I sometimes did this multiple times a day: connecting my feet to the ground, breathing energy into my still center, and breathing out to cleanse my aura and strengthen my edges.

Self Transformed by Sex: Devouring and Emergent

According to Paris Williams in his book *Rethinking Madness*, consciousness strives for a workable balance on the polarity between self-focus and other-focus.[31] Desire for autonomy and fear of engulfment drives us toward self-focus, in which we primarily attend to and value the concerns and preferences of self. Desire for intimacy and fear of isolation spurs us toward other-focus, occupied with the needs, concerns, and preferences of others. Somewhere between these drives lies our "window of tolerance," the amount of closeness or solitude we can tolerate.

Esoterically, we see this conflict on the Aries-Libra axis of Western astrology. Aries wants freedom, autonomy, delight in the joy of being. Libra wants harmony, connection, relationship, and balance in relationships. Aries risks rushing too far away from their secure foundation, too far out of the norm, and alienating their partners and allies. Libra risks forsaking their wants and needs indefinitely, putting others first with the unacknowledged expectation that the others will someday reciprocate. In both outcomes, parts get left behind: Aries's secret longing for connection and Libra's unstated needs and desires.

When self-focus moves too far afield of fears and desires around connection, the Gilded aspect of Egotism appears. A person in the inflated energy of Egotism is like a black hole, sucking in attention. Every topic relates back to their life or interests. If the conversation isn't about them, they'll find a way to bring it around. When having a conversation with someone in Egotism energy, you may notice frequent power games of getting into the one-up position and invalidation to put you in the one-down position. ("Oh, you visited Italy for a week? I once lived there for a year.") Though narcissistic folk appear to have quite a robust sense of self and self-validation, their egos are fragile. The slightest insult or invalidation throws them into a fury.

---

31. I am using the lowercase "self" to clarify that the self-other polarity is an egoic conflict. Self in the Iron Pentacle includes both polarities of the ego's self-other conflict.

The person in Egotism appears unable to speak or think of anything but themselves, but close attention reveals that there is no core of confidence or value therein, there is no sense of autonomy or self-containment. The person in Egotism is disconnected from their true values, deep desires, and unconscious motivations. Internally they might experience emptiness or numbness. They struggle to be present with themselves. Instead they fixate on others' responses, seeking attention, approval, and validation to maintain a sense of self. The way out of Egotism is to become curious and friendly toward the inner states, to shift identity from ego to Self.

Paris Williams asserts that beneath the vacillation between self and other is underlying unity. He points toward the experience of the non-dual, a state of no separation. I believe "unity" might alternately be named "dissolution." Williams illustrates this state with the analogy of a carrot being devoured. When I pick up a carrot, there is "me" and there is "the carrot." When I begin chewing the carrot, the carrot is no longer "carrot" but it's also not "not carrot." What was "carrot" is in a liminal state of devouring and absorption, after which stability is restored when it becomes part of "me."

The capacities to separate, merge, and re-emerge are facets of the dance between Sex and Self. During sex, the giving and receiving of sensations becomes an act with flow. During orgasm, ego boundaries soften, normal rules of cognition and awareness relax, and the brain is primed for rewiring. Sex magic harnesses this state with intention, directing that powerful energy to charge a working, fostering a change of consciousness to make possible the desired result.

The Divine Twins are 1 and -1, born from the 0 of God Hirself and uniting to form the Peacock.[32] On the personal level, the Self is our 0 from which the ego emerges as an individual unit, 1. Ego wants to say, "I am this!" but does so defensively, on some level aware that the -1 truth of "I am not this!" is also present.

The ego that wants to be seen as competent, beautiful, wise, for example, defends against those moments when it is helpless, ugly, and stupid,

---

32. Aleister Crowley discusses the occult formula of 0=2 in *Magick Without Tears*. In brief, 0=1 + -1; or 2 as in two integers.t.

though the Self includes all of these qualities. The -1, moreover, contains hidden potentials that strengthen and redeem the imbalances of the 1, not the least of which are compassion, self-acceptance, and humility.

The story of Nefertum evokes this experience through the emergence of the god and his immediate recognition of his aloneness, the negation of his being. The meeting of existence with this negation brings forth pain and the tears that birth humanity. This negation is highlighted in relationship to another creator god, Amun the "Hidden One." Before creation, some texts suggest that Amun existed in the dark waters of Nun in the form of a Cosmic Serpent, a form then discarded once the created world emerged. The discarded serpent form became jealous of Amun and the created world, and might be seen as the adversarial serpent who constantly seeks to undo creation and devour Re.[33]

Ego does not need to be eradicated, but rather exalted in service to God Soul. To do this, sometimes we must break up long-running patterns, deep wounds, and crystallized stories to which the ego clings. Sex, psychotherapy, and other forms of work on the Self facilitate this process. The process of purification or unbinding complexes allows us to dissolve these fixed facets and drink their energy back, so nothing is lost.

The following meditation offers one possibility for freeing up the energy stuck in crystallized patterns, beliefs, and stories about the Self:

Find a relaxing position for your body. With every inhalation, breathe into whatever is present in your body today—pain, tension, ease. With every exhalation, let your awareness sink more deeply into the body. Notice particular places where energy feels stuck or moves slowly through the body, but do not attempt to change anything now. Simply notice and expand your awareness.

Let your awareness sink into your heart. Call into your imagination a vision of the chambers of your heart, the terrain of your heart. Imagine yourself upon this terrain, walking its ridges and whorls.

---

[33]."The god Amun: Above All Reputation," *Shadows of the Sun*, 12 January 2013, https://warboar.wordpress.com/2013/01/12/pbp-a/.

There is a pit of darkness in your heart. Can you feel it? Can you sense it? Let yourself be guided to this place of darkness, the edge of the pit. What feelings arise as you gaze into this pit? Fear? Excitement? Anger? Joy?

This is the pit of devouring. What is dropped into this pit gets chewed up, dissolved, and merges with the darkness. This pit of darkness is a part of you, the raw material of your Self. What enters this pit may emerge in a new form, made of the darkness that is you.

What in you feels stuck? What story do you keep telling? What blind spot keeps arising? What tensions will not go away? Seek those within yourself, their symbols. Gather the symbols of these stuck parts, honor and acknowledge them. If it feels right, throw them into the pit. Notice how it feels to release these and allow them to be devoured.

You can end the working here, and return to your normal awareness. Or you may consider jumping into the pit. Does the darkness call to you? If you are willing, descend into the pit. Feel the darkness enfold and devour this facet of yourself. Keep breathing and relaxing your body as this happens. Let yourself dissolve into the dark.

What is in this pit with you? What lessons or allies dwell within? Be present in the dark. Let yourself be.

Finally, gather your awareness. Let this darkness be the material that becomes your new body. Form your body anew, and let it emerge from the pit of darkness. Thank yourself and the darkness within you, and breathe yourself back to your physical body, to your environment.

Self Exalted in Knowledge

Hail Djehuti, great of magic and insight;
Scribe of the gods, keeper of the archives,
Your eye has touched the data of the cosmos
And through Your mind all knowledge passes.
With Your mind bring stillness to undisciplined
Thought, that in silence we apprehend knowledge
In its countless facets. Turn Your blue lunar
Eye upon the darkness, illumine a new truth.

Once I was invited to draw a picture of Knowledge. What I came up with was an image of searchlights intersecting in the darkness at different angles. What this means to me is that Knowledge illuminates and yet limits. What we know is clear and obvious, but we may not appreciate that we only see one angle, one path in the darkness. We come to conclusions based on what we know within the context we understand, and later discover how much we got wrong.

Knowledge helps us to be effective. It offers ground against which we gain traction but that ground shapes what we think of as possible. The worst mistake is to think our Knowledge is complete and push away disagreement or conflicting data. I have witnessed deeply passionate, heated debates in which all participants react strongly and harshly to the other side's "ignorance" and imputed bad motives, centered on a particular piece of shared vocabulary. Few take the step back to make sure everyone agrees on the definition of the word. Many a tedious and draining argument could be avoided by defining terms.

Fighting over whose definition is correct and on which authority rarely leads anywhere useful. To illustrate this, consider a type of food well known across the United States, with very specific iterations. In Chicago, this food is often made with an all-beef frankfurter, poppy seed bun, yellow mustard, chopped white onion, sweet pickle relish, a dill pickle spear, tomato wedges, pickled peppers and celery salt. In Seattle, this food is made with several different types of sausage and toppings, has far fewer vegetables, and cream cheese smeared across the inside of the bun. Both of these cuisines are called "hot dogs."

People from Chicago who believe in their city's hot dog cannot fathom putting cream cheese or, for that matter, ketchup on a hot dog. Yet both recipes are valid. Each recipe reveals a unique facet of what is possible with the hot dog form, what variations of flavor. The distinction, and the passion in which some hold that distinction, invite curiosity about what in fact defines a hot dog.

I accrue Knowledge through the Self, and Knowledge in turn empowers me to express Self. When ruled by self-doubt I feel impeded in taking risks. In graduate school, I could write all kinds of papers and analyses of psychological phenomena and case studies of clients. I could listen to my peers and point out possibilities and insights. When I sat in front of an actual client, however, I felt frozen. I sat quietly, giving affirming noises, letting them know I was listening but unsure of how to respond. All my insight fled in the immediacy of the experience. All I could think was, "I don't know what to say."

When I brought this problem to my consult group, my instructor's advice was: "Say something." I had entangled myself with overthinking. What I needed to do was take a risk and connect with the client. As I got comfortable with taking action amidst not-knowing, I observed how the ensuing conversations deepened and expanded my understanding. I began to move from a removed, clinical theorizing toward an intimate, grounded, active sense of Knowledge.

Intellectual paralysis is a symptom of Knowledge without Self. One theory leads to the next and the next and we imagine we'll find a conclusion but none comes, for the realm of the mind is without end. We become lost in labyrinthine intellectual quests. The problem of Knowledge without Self is well-described by Aleister Crowley's description of the Qabbalistic Sephiroth Daäth (Knowledge) as containing "in itself the germ of self-contradiction and so of self-destruction. It is a false principle: for as soon as Knowledge is analyzed, it breaks up into the irrational dust of the Abyss."[34]

The Tarot suit of Swords offers a map of the journey into and out of disintegrated analysis paralysis. Each card is like a rung on the ladder of the body of Shu that separates and connects heavenly Nut and earthly Geb. What follows is one exploration of this journey, which could be read starting at the top (Nut), moving down the left column to the bottom (Geb), and then back up the right column to the top. In the spiritual journey, we could easily change course at any time, or hold the lessons of both pillars to manifest an integrative freedom.

34. Aleister Crowley, "Little Essays Toward Truth," *Hermetic Website*, http://www.bibliotecapleyades.net/crowley/littleessays/man.htm.

THE TAROT SUIT OF SWORDS & THE JOURNEY OF KNOWLEDGE

ACE OF SWORDS

The paradox of Knowledge as both a sharp, single-pointed instrument that cuts through bullshit and simultaneously the open, spacious nature of the *Mind That Knows*. The Knower and the Known are together, glittering as hard and cold as a diamond, rending the veils of illusion. If the Knower seeks to bring this Knowledge into manifest service, however, they must descend.

TWO OF SWORDS

The Knower sits between two irreconcilable and inescapable truths, separate from the holistic state of unity and blinded by dualism. The Knower cannot move forward while holding both, and worries they must discard one or analyze the paradox until a solution arises.

Having returned to the mystery of two, the Knower recognizes that dualism is false and useful. The two swords are one; are opposing poles of one. Though they appear irreconcilable, the Knower sits between in deep listening. Having bound the eyes, the Knower listens to intuition with the body's instinctive sense of holding the weight of the blades. Patiently, the Knower waits for the mystery to be revealed.

THREE OF SWORDS

Unable to reconcile the two certainties, the Knower finds a third truth. The bright, intoxicating cleanness of reason cuts through sentiment and muddy feeling troubling the mind's rootedness in the soul.

The Knower turns back toward their soul, and sees what parts have been cut away and buried in deference to reason. The intellect might be in service to the deep, mysterious messages of the soul; it might cleave the wound that lets the blood flow, or might withdraw and allow the soul to heal.

Four of Swords

Intellectual knowledge forms a coherent system of ideation, a theory that cuts free of the body. Indeed, the complexities of embodiment now seem an impediment to rational analysis, the accumulation of Knowledge, and the development of technology.

The Knower returns to the body through a practice of deepening and resting in silence. This feels at first like a sacrifice of the intellect, but it has been reversed. In sacrificing thought on the altar of the body, the Knower receives the deep insight of instinct and physicality. Knowledge returns to embodiment, to practice. Ideas no longer seem useful in of themselves and now must be tested for utility. Workability becomes more important than purity.

Five of Swords

Outside perspectives bring forward challenge with their own conflicting Knowledge, causing the Knower to respond defensively and aggressively, protecting their precious worldview. Having sacrificed heart and body on the altar of reason, the Knower looks upon the hurt they've caused with confusion, indifference, and scorn.

The Knower returns to the scene of fracturing and sees in each person a broken-away facet. Intellectualism was an escape from experiencing the parts of Self that fight, flee, or freeze. The Knower must claim all these pieces and integrate them. The question arises of being "right" versus being "connected." Each person holds a truth that might be honored without discord, division, and vitriol.

SIX OF SWORDS

Though the Knower continues to deepen in analysis and intellectual insight, they sense something is missing. They proceed on a journey into the unknown. Sitting upon a boat, the Knower seems to return cautiously to the intuitive realm, but through removed observation. The non-rational is a curiosity that seems to require scientific examination.

As the Knower reintegrates, their journey back across the water suggests a deep, expansive depression. All that has been rejected, wounded, and sacrificed in the search for Knowledge returns to the Knower. The temptation is to retreat into rationality, and the Knower needs an ally—a guide, a mentor, one who can help them cross this river.

SEVEN OF SWORDS

The Knower turns the accumulations of facts, information, and observations into an end of itself. Ethics, loyalty, and values of the heart and Spirit matter less than the task of increasing knowledge. Here is the scientist who conducts unethical experiments, the student who spends hours studying without thought for family or friends.

The Knower re-examines ethics. The shared community which the Knower has rejected in pursuit of pure intellectualism calls. The norms and needs of community as well as the pleasures and challenge of relationship call the Knower to connection and purpose.

EIGHT OF SWORDS

Trapped in a prison of mind, the Knower can rationalize away any act or conflicting desire, argue down any decision. They cannot move because every direction is fraught with imagined but seemingly rational dangers. Their intellectualism has become irrational, but the Knower cannot escape this.

Still conscious of the prison of mind, some part of the Knower, deeper than reason, feels the way to freedom. The river that wets their feet is the path out. They must walk it, though they cannot see or discern where the path will lead.

Nine of Swords

Worry substitutes for choice as the intellect becomes the realm of action. The physical world, so complex and foreign to the perfection of the intellectual imagination, becomes something to avoid or dominate. The living needs of the living Self become problems that need solutions. This state may well generate a wealth of life-enhancing technology and research: techniques to extend life, medications to address illness, and so forth.

The Knower strives to sit and listen to understand the mind, observe its constant seeking for solution. The Knower listens for silence between thoughts. Dreams and non-rational information erupt into consciousness, troubling the ego, guiding the Knower back to the Knowledge of the soul.

Ten of Swords

The nadir of Knowledge manifest in multiplicity, contradiction, and irreconcilable fragments. The Knower has expertise and intellectual authority but recognizes the limitations of the intellect in addressing the messiness of life. The Knower might feel overwhelmingly nihilistic, pinned to the world by too much rationality. Blood seeping from their wounds trails back toward the ocean, suggesting the pathway to integration. Intellectualism is not enough, and to become whole the Knower must turn toward the Knowledge accrued through intuition, instinct, and feeling.

For those of us who work with entities not necessarily perceivable by the physical senses, how do we know we are working with something "real," or an entity that is what it purports to be? Those who rebuild ancient cultus and actively work the courting of mystery examine the information we receive through personal gnosis against the information we have through research, academic study, and archaeology.

In a dream, I heard that "a god is a knowing subject who can itself be known," with the further implication that we know we speak with a god when that contact produces useful and new knowledge. I think it beneficial to keep an open channel to the information that comes to us through trance, astral journey, and personal contacts with gods and spirits. We also need practices to help us stay humble, connected to community, and critically examine the information we receive. Weighting personal gnosis too heavily creates the conditions for thoughtless, damaging actions and a loss of personal will. Too little faith in personal gnosis can cause us to defer to authoritarian leaders who claim to be the gates of tradition and knowledge.

One strategy of evaluating the validity of Knowledge is testing its efficacy in the world. Knowledge produces effects. "Technology" and "technique" share the root of "techno-", relating to skill, craft, systems, or art. Even when we do not fully understand the source or implications of Knowledge, we recognize we have something when derived techniques generate useful effects. A millennia ago, for example, Anglo-Saxons developed a recipe for an "eyesalve" that modern-day researchers have discovered is very potent in fighting MRSA.[35] The Anglo-Saxons did not share our modern context of germ theory, but their understanding clearly led to a technique that works. Knowledge encompasses both the observation of the technique and its effects as well as the theoretical reasoning or intuitions we have about "why."

Self is the cauldron in which information is gathered and cooked into Knowledge. When gods, spirits, ancestors, or miscellaneous contents of my unconscious provide a piece of insight or a technique, I hold it lightly while testing its reality. Parts of me are allowed to doubt the interpretation of my contact, even when external signs confirm the information I received. In this way, the transmutation of Knowledge involves the reception and study of non-rational information. Few of my intuitive guesses are easily turned into testable hypotheses, and I do not always understand what the information means to study it further. Even so, attending to results and confirmation helps us to recognize when we're dealing with something real.

All Knowledge, all experience, is contextualized and mediated by those factors that comprise the Self: history, culture, personal psychology, and politics. My position in the world, personal experience, and material reality

---

35. Nick Thompson & Laura Smith-Spark, "Thousand'year'ole Anglo-Saxon Potion Kills MRSA Superbug," *CNN Health*, 31 March 2013, http://www.cnn.com/2015/03/31/health/anglo-saxon-potion-mrsa/.

structures my searchlight. My experiences will lead me to notice facets that you do not. Such experiences mediate our encounters with Spirit, though Spirit itself likely transcends these.

Knowledge is the lexicon through which the gods and spirits may communicate with us. When our minds lack a certain piece of information or language, the gods and other spirits cannot discuss it with us. If they must, they will either help us re-create the concept; represent it through metaphor; or simply show us what they want us to know and leave it to us to spend the years trying to figure out what the hell it means. Imagine you don't know what a hot dog is, but I need you to make me one. Contemplate how that conversation would go, and then think of some of your more perplexing otherworldly contacts.

When Knowledge becomes too crystallized, we bind Spirit in constricting structures and codes. We find we have deified our techniques and fear the innate, destabilizing connection that gave rise to it. A blast of new insight obliterates the edifice, lightning striking the Tower.

When I started practicing magic, I had no idea what I was doing and to whom I should listen. Much of what I did, while sincere, are practices I would not now do. My beliefs have shifted, become more nuanced and refined, and entire pieces have dissolved or been thrown away. Yet my early magic was not bad or wasted. If I hadn't shown up and acted on what I knew then, I would not be where I am today. We must build the Tower so it may be destroyed, so that we may build a better Tower to be destroyed.

Clinging too rigidly to Knowledge keeps us from with that airy, expansive awareness that gives access to fresh perception and new information. The maxim, "As above, so below," offers a field of inquiry rather than a codified principle. What do my personal struggles tell me of the stories of the gods? How do the movements of planets in our solar system resonate with patterns of history? When I meditate upon the color red or the sigil of astrological Mars, what is my experience? What sensations, thoughts, emotions, or images emerge? What does this expression of Self reveal about the energy of Mars? Perhaps it is connecting to the above while it is the below that gives meaning, the Knowledge of who we are and why we live.

Water, Passion, Wisdom: Tides and Depths

Re learned that humans mocked him and plotted to arrogate his power. In anger, Re turned to Het-Her, cow-headed goddess of beauty, pleasure, and lust, who sat upon her dais enjoying the pleasures of the sky. "My precious Eye," said Re, "the gods are in danger from the humans. I need protection."

Het-Her sighed. "What human could be a threat to the gods? Cast these worries from your mind."

Re retired but fell into a sickness as his powers left him. He sent for Het-Her to witness his infirmity.

"The humans do this to me," said Re. "Do as I have asked. Protect the gods."

Enraged by the assault upon her beloved, Het-Her transformed into the lion-headed goddess Sekhmet, protector goddess of the sun's angry rays. She descended from the sky and with her might extinguished the would-be usurpers of Re. Their blood strengthened her thirst, and Sekhmet continued walking the human cities, killing and drinking their essence.

Upon recovery from his ailments, Re brought together his council of the gods. They feared Sekhmet would extinguish Kemet if she continued in her rage, but her might was such that none dared openly oppose her.

Ptah, however, had an idea. He brewed a dark red beer and poured it upon the earth, appearing like a river of blood in Sekhmet's path. The leonine goddess was overcome when she saw the river and sank to drink in the brew. Her rage ebbed. Her visage melting from vicious lion to the sweet-tempered cow. Sekhmet drank until she became Het-Her again, and peace returned to the land.

Passion is nourishment and relief to a parched soul. Passion breaks up stagnant and stuck energy. Passion draws toward a sense of connection and meaning in the world. Passion is mysterious, never to be mastered. Though at times I wish to be constantly engaged and excited, enthusiasm waxes and wanes. Passion and circumstance do not align as we would wish. Even when outwardly my life seems great, I experience feeling arid and dry, or suffused with that which feels toxic and unsettling. Other times when life looks chaotic, I feel rich with passionate energy. Passion keeps us moving, seeking, desiring. Passion unsettles even as it soothes.

WATER AND PASSION

When Passion is associated with Fire, we think of its enlivening and destructive qualities. Fiery passion lights up the world and animates, and yet it burns bright and hot, leaving ashes. When my teachers first suggested the association of Passion with water, I felt perplexed but intrigued.

Working with Passion as water connects me to a deep, cool, flowing relationship. Passion rises from below, pours down from above. Passion might be a drip, a trickle, a tiny stream of blood. Passion might be a tsunami that knocks us over with its force. Passion may be expansive and diffuse, or focused and fierce. Passion is cool water on a hot day. Passion is boiling water that cooks.

For the first several years in my work with the Iron Pentacle, the point of Passion felt the most distant and incomprehensible. Sometimes my energy would run toward my left foot and seem to dissolve into nothingness. Other times the energy seemed to "stop" before it got to my ankle. A trance journey with Passion gave me a vision of myself standing at the edge of an ocean, trying to float in the waves but constantly buffeted and knocked hard on the sand. Only when I saw myself standing and holding fast did I experience the waves flowing around me, tides shifting from high to low, while I remained grounded.

Will is the capacity to sustain committed action, to set an intention and act upon it. Our Work is our deep purpose in this world. Passion helps us discover our Work, but to access that we need to cultivate will. If all we do is react to the ups and downs of Passion, we will have great difficulty sustaining effort and developing the momentum needed to enact the larger projects of our Work. The excitement of discovery and falling in love with a new person, project, or idea lessens as the newness becomes more familiar and everyday. When our projects or relationships begin to show us unpleasant truths, we might be tempted to abandon the Work. Using will to stay the course in spite of these shifts, however, opens deeper reservoirs of Passion.

This relationship between will and Passion is illustrated by the metaphor of sailing a ship across the ocean. Will includes the work of checking the maps, orienting by the stars, and adjusting the sails and rudder to continue moving in the direction of desire. Passion is the ever-shifting climate: strong winds and steady currents one day, tempests the next, empty doldrums the next. We depend upon these elements and yet cannot control them. We must learn to do whatever is necessary to sustain the Work.

With practice, we learn how to work with these ups and downs. Doldrums offer the opportunity to do maintenance, preparing our vessel for the next gust of good wind. Tempests push us to learn how to endure, minimize harm, stay on course, and use that chaotic energy to keep us going.

Living with Passion means having a deep relationship with emotion itself. This includes more than simply what is considered "feeling good" or having "positive" emotions. All of our emotions have meaning, and repressing some while fixating on others deprives us of their power. More dangerous than painful feelings is stagnant emotion: for emotions that are not allowed to move and refresh themselves in contact with other feelings quickly become a toxic hindrance. A person who focuses only on "positivity" may find themselves unmoored when deep rage or grief arises. Another who prefers the "dark" emotions may run in terror from love and vulnerability.

Anger is one emotion that some folks are encouraged to have while others are punished for expressing. Those who are not allowed to feel and express anger lose its strength and self-asserting capacity. Those who are allowed to feel nothing but anger can only respond to hurt, embarrassment, and sadness with rage.

We find Passion in that which arouses profound caring, depth, and meaning. This might be a natural talent, love of a person, place, or cause, or an unexpected awakening of consciousness. Unexpected loss, becoming conscious of oppression, or profound grief and suffering might be the key that unlocks Passion. This latter pathway is embodied by "wounded healers" such as the centaur Chiron, who was gifted at curing all manner of illnesses and poisons except for the one with which he was afflicted.

Since I was seven, when I experienced an early depressive episode, I have been on a lifelong journey of seeking happiness. In recent years, I've come to see that "seeking happiness" is itself a source of unhappiness. The story of happiness as something to "seek" keeps it "out there" in a hypothetical future—a future when I'm thinner, or make enough money. I've come to see that happiness arises when I am in my life as it is. When I accept depression as a mood state that will change, I have an easier time remembering there is more to my life than sadness. This journey led me through witchcraft and into becoming a therapist, bringing to others the medicine I find healing. Without depression, I would not have discovered my Work.

The following exercise will help you to open up room for Passion:

Take some time in a quiet place to free-write about the following questions. You might set a timer for five minutes and let yourself write whatever comes to mind, then review and see what phrases feel charged to you.

What fills me with joy and gratitude? What breaks my heart? What troubles me? What fills me with enthusiasm?

When you review these writings, what qualities, tasks, values, or ideals seem most prominent? What connections exist between the things that trouble you and the things that fill you with enthusiasm?

Reflect upon these and work to develop a statement of Passion. Examples might be: "My passion is to foster beauty and justice." "I find passion in nourishing myself and others." "Passion leads me to craft suspenseful stories." "My passion is in my longing to know what I want." This does not have to be the end-all forever statement of passion, but one that captures your relationship with Passion today.

Once you have your statement of Passion, create a sigil. If you are familiar with sigil work, use your preferred method: magic squares, bindrunes, astrological sigils, and so forth. One simple approach is to write out your statement, cross out all repeat letters, and merge the remaining letters to create a unique symbol. Once you have your sigil, think of a spell that could bring this Passion into dimensions of your life that feel barren.

If the job you do for money feels devoid of passion, you might write the sigil on a place that you can look at it throughout your work hours to keep you connected. If you struggle to find passion at home, you might inscribe your sigil on a candle and spend some time each day meditating upon the candle flame.

For now, it's not necessary to make radical changes. Let the working lead you to new possibilities for integrating Passion into your life.

Passion Nourishing Sex: Expansion and Contraction

Running through the star, Passion is the last stop for Iron energy before it returns to Sex. Basic life force has undergone subtle changes and transformations and flows into the symbol-laden terrain of the soul, wherein mystery dwells, before again becoming distilled to its spiritual essence. This is the path of the artist, who listens deeply and remakes the world. Passion is the deep well of inspiration that calls us into this world.

Humans are creative. For whatever reason, it is not within us to leave well enough alone. We do not simply adapt to our surroundings; we shape our environment in subtle and profound ways. A tree branch could fall on the ground, rot, and return to the cycle of life, but a human senses within it the potential to become something else—a wand, a sculpture, a pencil. These creations encompass beauty as much as the discomfiting or confounding qualities of life. Passion leads us into realms of the mythic unconscious, inaccessible to the rational mind. Great art is a living entity unto itself, irreducible, producing new meaning and relationship. This is one reason that great art has its own life. Symbols and art are entities unto themselves. They resonate with depth and meaning. They produce new meaning and relationship with the changing world.

We live, think, and create within our cultural and historical contexts, informed by the Zeitgeist. Archetypal patterns and cycles act through us, as great and particular as the movement of the planets around the Sun. Through anchoring and exploring the particularities of the present moment, we touch the universal and timeless. In my experience, however, it does not work to move the other direction. Efforts to be "universal" tend to appeal to the norms and values of those who have economic and political power, while making invisible that specificity. Central figures of mainstream media tend to be heterosexual white men as the marketable "everyman" with which the audience is guided to identify.

Limitations, boundaries, and necessity are integral to the creative process. These qualities are associated astrologically with Saturn, the planet that speaks to the soul's constriction in the world of matter. When irreconcilable needs and obligations mire me, I want to innovate a new way of being or doing in the world. Without encountering limitation and sorrow, I have little motivation to create. Listening to my deep passion might feel threatening, with the potential to unsettle my comfort.

I want to express the pain and joy of my experience. Saturn teaches respect for limitations and the discipline that keeps me going. Saturn also corresponds to the materiality of the medium through which I create. The form of the poem, the material of the sculpture, the paints and brushes I choose, each of these energetically and materially shape the creative process.

Creativity also has expansive, buoyant qualities, associated with Jupiter's energy of the soul's empowerment in the world of matter. Jupiter opens new vistas of possibility and beauty. We innovate ways of doing work that free up time and energy for other passions. We create new kinds of medication or therapy, new philosophical innovations, a better way to organize the cooking supplies.

The higher revolutionary resonance of Uranus reminds us that innovations seemingly useless today prepare the way for something to come, as Farida Kachapova notes regarding "pure" mathematics: "Negative and complex numbers were regarded as absurd and useless before the 15th century. Now complex numbers are used in electrical engineering."[36] We cannot know whether the art we create today, in spite of self-doubts and thinking "this is a waste of time," will in some future time keep a vulnerable young person from committing suicide. We cannot know whether revolutions will rise based on the strength of a speech made with passion. When you do your work, results are not promised. No one can guarantee the visions of great wealth and social acclaim. Neither can we guarantee visions of universal scorn and failure. All we have is the inner journey and our relationship with life as it happens.

To explore your relationship to creativity, consider the following for reflection:

Whether you identify as an artist or not, spend some time thinking about what "creativity" means to you. When do you feel creative? What limits you? What possibilities invite you to expand?

PASSION EMPOWERED: KNOWING THE STAKES

Living with Passion, for me, means knowing what is at stake. I have fewer emotional defenses. I feel my joys more joyfully, I feel my heartache more sorrowfully. What I do matters, and I am increasingly more aware of how and why it matters.

---

36. Farida Kachapova, "On the Importance of Pure Mathematics," *Journal of Mathematics and Statistics*, Volume 10, Issue 14.

A low-stakes life without Passion looks like one inhibited by fears of how others will respond. I may choose a career or a spouse based on family expectations. I may silence my voice in response to outrage over racism because I fear consequences from my friends or my co-workers. I may swallow my anger and desire to act because I'm convinced nothing will make a difference. When these emotions—energy that wants to move and act in the world—are stymied, swallowed, or blocked in expression, we either act out or start numbing, leading to the Gilded quality of Apathy.

Apathy is a state of listlessness, numbness, aimlessness, emptiness. Apathy might also look like a state of comfort to which we cling rigidly, avoiding any threats to comfort. A person in Apathy will find any reason to quell the impulse that threatens to disrupt the status quo.

Apathy may present rational, air-tight arguments as to why a desired action is a bad idea or wouldn't matter in the long run. We may hear Apathy as though it is a trusted sage that keeps us safe, at the mere cost of living a full life. So persuasive is this voice that we miss the holes in the arguments, the unearned certainty, the unproven assumptions. To be sure, Apathy is not always sanguine—to others, it may come out as an abusive, toxic voice that defensively shuts down every desire.

In my telling of the Kemetic story at the start of this chapter, Het-Her appears to be in a state of Apathy. Re's efforts to rouse her to action end up absorbed in her sloth. Comfort, beauty, and leisure take priority over the looming, distant threat. Only when the situation sinks into her heart does it activate will.

One of Apathy's tricks is convincing us that our actions increase security and avoid risk. Het-Her illustrates the problem of privileged folk who intellectually understand there are problems affecting "other" people. Those problems may bother the privileged in the abstract, but letting those problems get too close to the heart feels risky. If I give up what I have now and really care about these distant problems... well, something bad could happen. I could lose what I have. But the only thing I can be certain I'll lose is this beguiling complacency.

Another word for "knowing what's at stake" is risk. To feel is to risk. When I turn toward what has heart and meaning for me, I become more aware of my feelings about it. I truly encounter the obstacles, discouragement, feelings of powerlessness, and disappointment. I experience the moments of elation, breakthrough, success, joy, or connection. Not all at once, but my capacity for each continues to expand. Powerful expressions arise from vulnerability and courage. Sharing from this place feels rich and deep, though at times painful for both the sharer and the witness. Pastor Nadia Bolz-Weber speaks to this when she says that she preaches "from my scars, not from my wounds."[37] My interpretation of this is that an open wound lacks containment and would be unsafe to share in public expression, spreading trauma instead of healing it. A scarred experience, however, is rich in emotional content yet contained in body and soul.

Imagine sitting with a group of people you have known for a long time—friends, coworkers, family, people in your spiritual community—and something occurs that bothers you. Someone behaves with disrespect. They say something that goes against your deep values. Imagine that, unlike all the other times when you've let the moment pass, today you decide to speak. Imagine the rush of energy in your heart and limbs, the lift of anxiety and adrenaline meeting for this work. Imagine the feeling of fear inside as you prepare to acknowledge the truth of the matter. You don't know what will happen next. You might be wholly ignored. You might be ridiculed. You might be exiled. People might agree with you. People might approach you and thank you for your courage. You might reach a new understanding of each other. You might find that whatever happens next is more tolerable than you had imagined.

This is a moment rich with Passion. Whatever happens next, you are in contact with your felt sense of what is at stake. Moving with these feelings is different from impulsive reaction. Lashing out in anger, shrugging off others, and throwing blame around is not consciously aware of what's at stake.

---

37. Krista Tippett and Nadia Bolz-Webber, "Seeing the Underside and Seeing God: Tattoos, Tradition, and Grace," *On Being*, 23 October 2014, https://onbeing.org/programs/nadia-bolz-weber-seeing-the-underside-and-seeing-god-tattoos-tradition-and-grace/.

In relationship to Passion, all of your parts attend to the moment and move forward with a powerful choice, able to respond to whatever consequences occur.

We have to learn the difference in how these states feel, which requires practice and self-observation. That first daring act often feels clumsy and inspires feelings of shame and regret. You will fail. Failure is integral to learning to succeed. You'll learn, however, what seems to work and what does not work. This expands your efficacy, and your capacity to experience and work through your feelings. With practice, you may find that your voice has more power than before. Your actions attract more notice and connection. People who seemed indifferent or hard to move begin to listen to you, in ways you never would have expected. Unexpected allies appear.

For some, anxiety is debilitating and they need professional support to develop skills and capacities to manage it. Anxiety says things like: "They'll think you're crazy. You're not ready to do this. You will fail. Go calm down and then you can try. Maybe take a few more classes. You don't really need this anyway. It's not worth the risk." We have anxiety about things that matter to us.[38] Avoiding anxiety only temporarily relaxes its hold.

Anxiety looks like an obstacle to desire, but it is more like the gatekeeper. Our avoidance is what gives it power. When we look more closely, however, it does nothing to stop us from passing through the gates. We only need the strength to tolerate that anxious discomfort while following through. Such strength comes with practice.

As someone with an anxious mind, I notice sometimes my anxiety is "about" something and sometimes it seems to shift from topic to topic indiscriminately. I might be in a bad mood and under-slept, and if my husband responds to a text message without an appropriate emoji I start to wonder if he's secretly angry with me. Historically I would dwell upon this fear for hours, or tell other people about the situation and ask if they think the person's upset.

⟆⟇⟆

38. Here I am speaking of the general experience of anxiety, and not specific phobic experiences or anxiety related to traumatic wounding, although these experiences too may bar the path to desire when avoided.

Finally I started a practice of approaching the person directly to check in and choosing to believe what they say. Rather than accusing them of having the feeling I fear, I note my observations and ask them to tell me how they feel. When listening, I do my best to hear where they are coming from without defending or justifying myself. Trust builds when we approach problems honestly and without defensiveness. Allowing the other to have an opportunity to act in good faith helps me to discover how trustworthy they are.

Moving toward anxiety enlivens us. There is nothing more relieving than finally having the conversation I've been afraid to have, or doing the thing that terrifies me. All those hours of avoidance feel draining and suffused with doom and terror. In the moment of stepping up with heart-filled passion, I feel a kind of grace takes hold and carry me through the experience.

The following reflection and exercise will support you in naming and doing those life-affirming acts you might avoid:

What words do you often think but never speak? What action do you often think you want to take but never do? What event do you want to attend but often postpone?

Observe these patterns in yourself for the next week. Notice the times when you talk yourself out of taking action. Notice those moments when you seem to "blank out" or feel unexpectedly blocked from taking an action that means something to you. Notice those situations that arouse strong feeling, and spend some time with the feeling.

The following week, notice those times when you act impulsively. Notice when and how often you express your feelings. Notice when you seem to be talking a lot. Do you feel connected in these moments? Are you able to meet the eyes of those around you? Do these words, actions, and feelings seem to support the life you want to create?

Perhaps outwardly it looks like you are an emotionally expressive person but internally you feel numb and disconnected, or vice versa. How could you bring that explosive energy into the service of what gets suppressed? How could you bring that containing energy into the service of what leaks out?

Contemplate the various ways humans have learned to harness the power of water: the waterwheel, the plumbing system, the lock system, the dam, the aqueduct, the irrigation canal. What tool might help you to harness your passion? Like water, passion needs to flow.

What step would feel daring? Take a small but meaningful risk based on the work above.

Passion Balancing Pride: Flow

Both Passion and Pride are located in the feet. They connect us to the ground of our being. For those who are able to walk with both feet, weight and energy shifts from one to the other. They support stabilization and movement in ongoing adjustments to the terrain. I suggest that the metaphysical function of the curve between Passion and Pride is similarly involved in the dynamics of movement and stability, rhythm and pace.

Kemetic depictions of the gods and pharaohs often position them with left foot stepped forward, right foot back. Monica Bowen, art historian and professor, suggests that this evokes the left side of the body, where the heart resides.[39] The heart, or Ab, in the Kemetic worldview was the seat of emotions, consciousness, will, and personality. According to our current understandings of neurobiology, the right lobe of the brain controls the muscles on the left side of the body, and the characteristics of what is processed in this lobe includes creativity, holistic and symbolic thinking, intuition, rhythm, feeling, and non-verbal communication. The left foot, therefore, could be leading into mystery while the right foot grounds the being in the rational and linear.

Our right-brain features take priority in childhood before training in logic, productivity, and language shift us to the left. Children work through feelings and complex problems through play and imagination. In the

---

39. Monica Bowen, "Ancient Egyptians and Greeks: Left Foot Forward!" *Alberti's Window*, 22 May 2014, http://albertis-window.com/2014/05/ancient-egyptians-and-greeks-left-foot-forward/.

United States, however, these traits get locked in their association with childhood and most of us are expected to set aside the non-rational when we become adults, instead prioritizing the linear, logical, productive, and profitable. The internalization of Capitalism leads us to measure our feelings through standards of productivity. "There's no point to feeling sad."

This has a significant impact on magic workers and the spirit-sensitive. Those who have learned to devalue the right brain and overvalue the left brain express impairment in their ability to utilize psychic senses and employ magic; or they may be so convinced that they're impaired that they overlook very real psychic experiences. Those whose right brains and sensitivities are highly developed struggle to meet the demands and expectations of mainstream culture. They might be the subject of scorn and dismissal. The non-rational terrifies mainstream culture.

The connection between Passion and Pride supports us in affirming the validity and power of our subjective, intuitive, emotional experiences. As we practice magic, listen to the messages of noncorporeal beings, and do the work those insights call us toward, we become more attuned to the holistic, synchronicity-rich dimension of the world. We become less afraid of working with intuitive guesses or putting psychic understandings out in the world. We follow Passion to create, not knowing what the outcome will be. We might learn to better understand and trust our emotions, instincts, and intuitions.

We can become unbalanced, however, in overvaluing our emotions and the non-rational at the expense of other parts of self. This is the Gilded state of Obsession, which in this context is related to words like "fascination" and "addiction." The person in Obsession becomes fixated on a particular experience of emotional intensity, underlying which is often an effort to escape from an unwanted reality. A person in Obsession is trying to move toward the ecstatic experience without the simultaneous movement inward to ground and integrate the experience in their life. This leads to increasingly violent patterns of getting "high" on the Obsession and crashing "down" to the mundane-feeling reality.

For some, there is something in the self that feels oppressive, upsetting, or souring that we find freedom from when engaged in the Obsessed activity. Perhaps I feel awkward and uncomfortable trying to socialize with people, but when I go home to my altar I can trance for hours and cavort with gods and demons, feeling all-powerful. Obsession might look like spending more and more time in this exciting, exalted state of being and avoiding any social contact that would make me uncomfortable.

Left unchecked, Obsession takes increasingly more resources from other aspects of life. Relationships suffer. Health suffers. The money we should spend on rent goes toward the Obsession. Eventually we wake to realize that we no longer experience any pleasure or fulfillment in the Obsession. We have been made into its servant. We spend our life force feeding it.

In the story that opened this chapter, the goddess Sekhmet expresses this energy of Obsession, having been roused to a passionate defense of Re. Her destructive actions exceeded what the circumstance needed, detached from her guiding values. She was caught in the doing, in the thrill and intoxication of the act itself.

The solution that pacified Sekhmet, a river of blood-colored beer, offers a symbolic clue to Obsession's antidote. The river appeared to Sekhmet as the perfect object of her desire. What it led her to do, however, was to slow down and remember that which had been lost in her Obsession. Ease, pleasure, and gourmet indulgence brought her back to the form of Het-Her. Her Obsession had become a warped mirror of Passion; instead of luxuriating in the pleasures of this world, she luxuriated in its annihilation. Instead of feeding her own life force through connection, she fed upon others'.

Passion brings us vitality, but Obsession becomes destructive escapism, bypassing what feels boring or painful without resolving them. Boredom and "mundane" activities have a grounding function. Sometimes the tide of Passion is high, and other times it feels at an ebb, and we can be present to it all.

In some respects it is a relief to have moments in life that are not so heavily weighted, in which we're simply doing laundry and not something profound and hugely impactful. A life of being useful, thoughtful, and living to our best abilities may be a simple, easy, quiet life. Passion is not always loud and bold.

Take a moment to check in with your Passion:
Pause right now and notice your body. Notice your breath. Where do you feel your Passion in this moment? Where does Passion dwell in your body? What in your surroundings connects you to Passion? What parts of your life could use attention and energy today? Think about a beloved hobby you haven't done, need or desire you haven't addressed in a while. What could you do today to feed that facet of Passion?

Passion Deepening Self: Connecting to Emotion

One possible way of looking at emotional problems is to see them arising from difficulty accessing, containing, or expressing feelings. Those three processes—access, containment, and expression—comprise the emotional system. Access is our ability to sense and understand what we are feeling. Containment is our power to be present with the feeling and inhibit reactive impulses. Expression is our capacity to share the feeling with others. Each process contributes to a healthy emotional system. Excessive or deficient functioning in one process affects the others.[40]

A deficiency in access is like having no water source whatsoever, or one that is hardly a trickle. It might show up as emptiness, numbness. This is a symptom of several mental disorders, including depression and dissociative disorders arising from trauma. In these, the processes of containment and expression are difficult to assess. When feeling does occur, the person suffering may express it in dissociated episodes of rage or sadness. It looks like intense emotion, but the person experiences their consciousness as disembodied or wholly absent from the experience. The person might begin

---

40. I am thankful to Anodea Judith for discussing the concepts of "excess" and "deficiency" as energetic problems in her book on the chakras, *Eastern Body, Western Mind.*

weeping uncontrollably but describe it as a "bodily release" without emotional content.

An excess of access would be like having a waterfall or river rapids as your water source; more than enough, but dangerous. A person with excessive access is easily overwhelmed and frequently acts upon feelings without thinking of consequences. Examples of excess include anger spurring harmful words and actions toward others or towards themselves, gleefulness causing one to overlook red flags in a relationship, or sadness spurring self-numbing behaviors.

The process of containment relates to the magical tool of the cup in its power to hold. The above examples of excessive access also relate to a deficiency in containment. Because there is no inner capacity to contain, people with this deficiency might be preoccupied with blaming outside people and circumstances for their problems or using a variety of strategies to control others' feelings. These strategies range from emotional withholding, threats, and intimidation to "nicer" strategies of placating, people-pleasing, or derailment. Those with a deficiency in containment might fall back to self-numbing or self-harming behaviors to gain some kind of control, damaging health and relationships.

A person with an excess of containment tends to appear aloof, cold, and insensitive, but is internally flooded by intense emotional experiences that threaten their rational faculties. A person like this tends to have grown up in an environment in which they became convinced that showing their feelings was unsafe and would lead to exploitation or harm. Because they lack the inner skills to manage emotions effectively, they engage in avoidance of places and situations that might elicit the threatening feelings. When flooded they may go into "stonewalling," hardening the exterior and appearing to have no reaction. They may experience themselves as easily hurt or upset, but the people around them may have no idea that this is happening.

Expression is another facet of the cup, its capacity to pour. Deficiency in containment tends to correlate to an excess of expression, and vice versa. If I cannot hold my emotions, I tend to splash them all over the place and rely on others to help me manage them. If I hold my emotions too firmly, then I tend to be disconnected from others and lose access to the healing, connection, and intimacy of sharing.

With self-observation, you may be able to identify your overall tendencies in these emotional processes. You may also discover that these processes vary with certain emotions, with some more easily contained and others more easily expressed, and still others seemingly beyond access.

Emotions have physical as well as energetic expressions; they inspire changes in the body related to their instinctive function. Fear makes us cold because the body moves blood to the arms and legs, spikes us with adrenaline, and makes us ready to run away. Anger is similar, preparing us to fight off a threat. Sexual desire causes well-known changes in preparation for intercourse: the penis, clitoris, nipples, and vulva become more sensitive and engorged. Disgust elicits bodily responses of closing off to or expelling the disgusting stimuli.

Emotions are also communications from the soul, conveying deeper information about the Self's experience and relationship to environment and purpose. It is useful to distinguish between emotions and our thoughts about the emotions—the story we tell, the beliefs we have. This distinction is often blurred. English speakers in the United States use "I feel..." as a beginning to a sentence that expresses an opinion, belief, or intuitive guess. "I feel" may relate to the emotions, but frequently it is a story about the emotion or an allegation about the situation. "I feel you are trying to sabotage me," for example, is very different from "I feel disrespected and scared."

Emotions are not rational. When we understand them through rational stories, we miss out on the depth of communication. If I feel excessively angry and think it is because this person did not call me at the time we agreed, I miss the possibility that the anger is also saying I'm exhausted and resent this entire project and need to withdraw. Or I might be picking up on someone else's anger and treating it as mine.

What helps is practicing the capacity to notice and be present with emotion itself, holding our stories at abeyance while listening. The more we can notice the subtle fluctuations of feelings in the body—what psychologist

Eugene Gendlin calls the felt sense—the greater our understanding of what the emotion "means."[41] My interpretation of the feeling is often a guess. When I tell a story about my feeling, my body feeds back about the accuracy of my guess. When I truly name the cause of my feelings, I notice a sense of relaxation and rightness. When I am on the wrong path, I notice an increase in tension and distress.

Emotions are much like pets or nonverbal children. They have needs and desires and have not learned to communicate in a language that the rational mind understands. Ignoring their needs or pleas for attention increases the distress, and the creature might act out or throw tantrums to get us to sit down and listen. Much of our social training says that "discipline" means not "giving in" to these tantrums and instead focusing on punishing the acting out behavior, which means the creature's needs and capacity for self-assertion become subsumed or redirected to some behavior that is more palatable for the caregiver. This solution becomes toxic.

When our feelings "act out" through behaviors that hurt self or others, it is appropriate to set limits and attempt to reduce the harm, but that is incomplete. The nonverbal creature's acting out and distress may be in large part a fear that the caregiver upon whom they depend for survival is not attuned to their needs and safety. Turning toward the distress and connecting reduces that fear, and then we can listen more deeply to what the emotion is trying to communicate.

Such communications are best approached as symbolic. The experience of the symbol is ineffable; speaking of the experience is necessarily unable to communicate the fullness of the experience. To encounter a symbol with an expectation of what it will be is to limit our capacity of discovering the more that it could be. Thus, with feelings I want to ask questions that open up possibilities, like "What is this anger communicating right now?"

---

41. Eugene Gendlin, *Focusing* (New York: Bantam Dell, 1978).

The following exercise supports this journey:

Find a relaxed posture in a place where you feel safe and won't be disturbed. Slow down your breathing, and check in with your body. Notice the flow of energy, where in your body there is tension and ease. Breathe into your center and exhale, allowing space to open up inside. Notice if any strong emotions feel present right now. If so, work with these emotions. If not, then recall a recent event that was emotionally distressing. Call into your awareness as much detail as you can recall—what was said, what you felt, what the environment felt like, what you heard.

Notice what emotions and sensations are present. If you can, name them. "I am noticing anger. I am noticing tension. I am noticing sadness. I am noticing a pain in my stomach."

Focus your awareness on one of these strong sensations. Notice the parts of you that might resist or distract you from this work. Acknowledge them and attempt to bring your attention back to the emotion. If the feelings of resistance are particularly strong, however, you would be well served to use this as your focus.

Imagine that you, the larger You, can turn toward this part of you that is feeling this strong emotion with kindness and curiosity. Say hello to this part. Let it know that you are here with it.

Take a blank piece of paper and art materials and create an image of this part of you that has this feeling. What colors, symbols, words, or phrases go with this part of you? What is its name? Once the symbol is complete, breathe into the feeling and send its energy into the image.

Now you can have a dialogue with this part of you. Ask it what it's trying to communicate, and record the answers as they come to mind. Avoid thinking about the answers and try writing whatever comes to mind, no matter how strange or obvious it may seem. Invoke curiosity and kindness in trying to understand the worldview and needs of this part of self. You might also tell this part of you your challenges in dealing with it, and asking the part how you could have a better relationship. If the part of you suggests a practice to follow, take special note of this and make a contract to try this, so long as it will be safe for your whole self.

Once you feel complete, breathe the energy from the symbol back into yourself. Do what you will with the image, but I discourage you from attempting to destroy or "bind" the part of self with the image.

Passion Exalted In Wisdom

Hail Neith, self-created, self-birthed,
You are the very waters of fecundity
And annihilation, you are the heartbeat
And the dance of the hunt, the arrow
Flying toward the heart's desire,
The blood of prey loosed in steam
And heartache. In Your great love
You nurse to life what will die,
You know the ache of the living,
You contain the uncreated chaos,
You bear the source of life, Re,
You bear his nemesis, the serpent,
You weave together our threads,
Your great Eye sees the patterns.

When I was younger, people thought me wise. An "old soul." Much of this, I think now, came from being an emotional support to my family during its dissolution at an age that now seems far too young. When it came to friends' family and relationship dramas, I had answers to offer. When it came to my life, I lived in depressive emptiness, anxiety, and self-hatred. I feared missing out while rarely being courageous enough to step up. Did I truly possess Wisdom?

If it was Wisdom, it was drunk from a shallow cup. Other people's problems are always easier to solve than our own. Our own problems seem deeply complex and confusing and the reductive simplicity of outside advice feels dismissive. We think our view is clear standing above a person, but getting in the mud with them helps us understand why they're stuck.

Wisdom is in the mud. Wisdom endures scalding, wounding, healing, joy, rejection, success, and failure. Wisdom is attunement to rhythm and current, seeking efficacious choices based on the information at hand. Wisdom guides action, arising from our innate sense of meaning and connection. A wise course of action is not necessarily without pain, but it will move toward pain purposefully, suffer intentionally.

Some Pagans I've known take exception to my use of the word "suffering." For Pagans, pain might be accepted and worked with as necessary, but suffering suggests attachment to misery-provoking circumstances and should be ended when possible. They attribute the notion of suffering as enduring pain because one "deserves it" to more problematic strains of Christian thought. What is more usefully contained within the Christian view is suffering as purification of the soul, teaching us to release what causes us harm.

To G. I. Gurdjieff is attributed the aphorism, "Only conscious suffering has any sense." This suggests suffering as an active, transformative experience. Suffering consciously, we observe our pain and its roots that we may more effectively heal it. This method has proven results through the work of people like John Kabat-Zinn, who introduced mindfulness meditation to the treatment of chronic pain in Western psychology. This approach epitomizes conscious suffering, in which participants set aside painkillers and practice presence and self-observation amidst the pain. The practice does not eradicate pain but instead befriends it, decreases the aversion and hatred of it, which decreases the overall stress and anxiety felt about it. Pain stops being a problem to solve at all costs, and participants feel more freedom as a result.

When we are unwilling to experience our lives in total, we create more suffering for ourselves. People are excellent at coming up with strategies to get away from the unpleasantness of life, and so many of these strategies create unwanted consequences such as: empty bank accounts, hangovers, ruined relationships, physical ailments, apathy, emptiness, and loneliness. I have met people who assuage painful anxiety with regular marijuana use, leading to feeling disconnected and numbed out. Reducing the use of the substance terrifies, not least because now they've lost what skills they had to manage anxiety without cannabis. They are caught in a dilemma: continuing pouring money and time into a habit that disconnects, or confronting the pain and discomfort of reconnecting. [42]

Our inner complexes confine, restrict, inhibit, or drain the current of Wisdom. We make choices because other people want us to, or we cut corners because we're tired, even if the wise part senses that these momentary compromises will have long-term consequences. Wisdom at times feels cold, a loving nonattachment that erodes illusion and our grasping and needing.

In life, we choose our suffering. We suffer the consequences of avoidance, or we suffer our authentic experience. How's that for a motivating call to action? Yet suffering from avoidance shuts things down, leaves us feeling passive or resentful. Suffering our authentic experience, as painful as it is, is life-affirming. Conscious suffering yields the deep understanding of the experience of being in this world and doing our Work. When we feel burnt out or resentful, conscious suffering leads us to the fresh springs of integrity, sweetness, and joy.

Distilled Wisdom challenges rationality through poetry, aphorisms, paradox, or simple statements that upend preconceptions. This Wisdom lives because it evades reduction, it cannot become a rigid and arid set of

---

42. This is not a blanket judgment on marijuana use for medical reasons. You know better than I what feels life-enhancing and what feels numbing for you.

rules. It spurs contemplation. At the same time, Wisdom makes sense because it resonates with every part of us. Intellect, body, feeling, values, and will each flow together into the wise action, the profound insight, thus we recognize it with our whole being. A felt sense of rightness, of "yes" unfolds in the body. A wise choice pushes me past comfort and stagnation, though not always into discord, confusion, and doubt.

Tracing Wisdom along the Body of Shu, we might look at the descending path as attachment and the ascending path as nonattachment. In Western psychology, "attachment" is an important and necessary component for the development of identity, emotional regulation, and healthy forms of relationship. It begins in our primary bonds with our caregivers, which form the template for our basic sense of trust and safety in the world. Nonattachment comes from the influences of Buddhism, Hinduism, and other "Eastern" spiritual traditions, as the process of releasing our egoic desires to cling, to fix, to attach our happiness to what is truly impermanent. The Tarot cards of the suit of Cups offer an illustration of these paths. A person might start from the Ace, descend to the Ten, and then ascend to the Ace, or might switch paths frequently, or attempt to walk both.

THE TAROT SUIT OF CUPS & THE JOURNEY OF WISDOM

ACE OF CUPS

The Seeker is immersed in connection and Wisdom, attuned to the rhythms of God Hirself. The Seeker is the drop and the ocean, complete and whole in the fullness and depth of experience. In this state, as a totality, the Seeker is somewhat removed from world and connection with others. The Seeker may long for both separation and connection, to know their depths through experience.

TWO OF CUPS

The Seeker experiences the pain of separation and the delight of connection. They see in another what they perceive to be absent in themselves: the possibility of joy. In intense connection, the Seeker and their lover may attempt to merge or make each like the other, hoping to minimize unhappiness.

The Seeker connects with others and delights in the opportunity to see themself mirrored in relationship. Intimacy is another crucible of learning Wisdom, learning more about the Self, even in moments of pain and loneliness. The Seeker strives to wholly accept self and wholly accept other without attempting to change anything.

THREE OF CUPS

The tension and upheaval of the dyad seeks relief through triangulation. Together, their joy is more joyful, their sorrow more sorrowful. The Seeker sees that one person cannot be the sole mirror, that each relationship brings out unique facets and deficits.

Having discovered a deeper sense of Wisdom and meaning, the Seeker delights in every experience available. All people are kin, all feelings are beautiful, and joy is possible in every moment.

Four of Cups

The Seeker experiences loneliness and depression, and contemplates why their relationships feel not enough. They long for the transcendent connection of the Ace but each relationship is as flawed as it is wonderful. The Seeker turns inward, sinking through the pain of loneliness and disconnection. They feel purpose and divinity are far away, too far to be helpful.

Contemplation of pain and depression enables the Seeker to receive divine insight. They discover the connection that is possible in every moment, the larger connection to deity or the rhythms of the world. Loss and gain, happiness and sorrow, all are part of the secret.

Five of Cups

The Seeker falls deeper into depression, longing for meaningful connection to the world. The Seeker fears that pain and heartache are signs of failure, and happiness a sign of Wisdom. They can only focus on what they've lost, how they've failed, and struggle to remember what blessings are still available to them.

The Seeker deepens into long-held sorrow and pain, connecting to grief about the impermanence of the world. Even this pain they perceive to be necessary, to contain deeper Wisdom. They no longer turn away from darker sensations.

Six of Cups

Spring returns to the Seeker's heart, represented by the flowering cups. The Seeker takes refuge in contemplation, work, and service, searching for happiness through beauty and being of service to others.

The Seeker turns toward contemplation, play, and nature. Work is about service and connection and not about reward, status, or personal gain.

SEVEN OF CUPS

The Seeker becomes enamored of dreams with great success and failure. Wealth, fame, and status join with love as the outward signifiers of happiness that the Seeker desires.

Fantasies and dreams now seem like strange illusions to the Seeker, things that may outwardly spur movement and purpose but ultimately veil the truth of their heart. The Seeker knows these fantasies come from something deeper.

EIGHT OF CUPS

The Seeker either accomplishes one of the fantasies of the Seven or fails in the attempt. Regardless, they realize that possessing the cup is not the same as filling the cup. Meaning and happiness seem impossible to find in current conditions.

The Seeker may turn away from the outer trappings of happiness and wealth to go on a journey into the depths and darker emotions. The Seeker no longer thinks of happiness as the sole purpose in life, instead seeing the full range of experience as part of the mystery they wish to explore.

NINE OF CUPS

Turning inward, the Seeker rediscovers the wellspring of Wisdom and joy. They realize their capacity for the totality of experience, and their independence. The Seeker is able to generously and fully attach to the world.

The Seeker begins to explore their sense of self apart from their relationships. They stay involved in life as it is but begin to look at their role in long-term, unsatisfying patterns. They explore the mystery of changing others by changing self.

TEN OF CUPS

The Seeker manifests joy and wealth through relationships, not fixated on what they can receive but instead what they can give. They find their completion through knowing themselves and supporting others in the work of living. Even this, however, may leave them restless, particularly as these relationships continue to change and evolve. The Seeker still experiences themselves as alone and wishes for a deeper connection to the source of meaning.

Living according to another person's version of reality divorces us from our own psychic roots. Every piece of Wisdom should be welcomed with curiosity until we reach the moment where we sense its truth in our own experience. If something in my work touches you and resonates with truth, that is your connection to Wisdom.

Following a practice requires a certain amount of context and teaching, but the practice itself is what leads us to Wisdom. Telling myself, "I must be kind to others at all times" without a practice that encourages compassion tends to mean that I am running myself from an intellectual, rule-bound place. The Inner Critic will always find reasons to tell me why I'm doing a bad job being kind, or how I wasn't kind enough, and at times that will all fall away and I'll find myself acting like a shithead because this person *really* deserves it and I don't really know *why* it's so important to be kind.

Instead of taking that as a rule, I could accept kindness as a practice that teaches. I commit to practicing kindness this week. There is no "should" or "ought" here, no moral imperative, no sense that I'm going to be punished for failing to follow the practice. I am going to try it, and see what it's like.

So I practice and find my heart softening. I notice how much more gentle and alive I feel, and how others respond to me with greater sensitivity and ease. Subtle shifts happen that don't make sense. People smile with surprised delight or cry in unexpected gratitude. Something within me opens and shifts, and I realize I like acting this way. Then I go back to my spiritual books and read on the virtues of kindness and find my experience of reading has changed. The words are the same but I understand differently. What it's saying speaks to me, to the part that has experienced the teaching, and now the words penetrate and sink deeper. When I encounter people who piss me off and hurt me, I have kindness as an option and not a commandment.

We may take this approach with spiritual texts. Instead of accepting them as truths beyond personal reckoning, they might be symbolic doorways to enter through practice. Take a trance journey to the world of the symbol. Hold the esoteric phrasing in your soul parts and walk through the worlds, noticing what occurs. Let a practice emerge. Get an inner sense of how the teaching works.

Energetic transmission from those who embody the Wisdom we seek is a powerful and time-honored form of teaching. Living, human teachers with whom you can meet in person are excellent for this purpose. Using our tools of ritual and trance to connect to spiritual entities is another excellent resource. Practicing in community, even more profound. Water's rhythmic quality shows up when we synchronize in community. With close connection, several drummers will naturally fall into a shared rhythm, a process called entrainment. Heartbeats join together. Menstrual cycles match. So, too, will energetic and emotional states oscillate in time with those around us. Connection to a strongly centered and ass-kicking teacher helps us to oscillate in more optimal ways.

As much as I value the rhythms of my daily practice, I need community—in-person connection—to call me back to the core of my practice. Solitary practice is not inferior to group practice—indeed, it can avoid some of the pitfalls of groups and be vastly less stressful—but humans seem to be wired to do our deepest work in groups. My meditations and trance journeys are never so clear and deep as they are when I am in community. Community confronts me with the material that I need to work on to become more myself in this world. My colleagues give me useful feedback, reveal their own Wisdom gained from the work, and challenge me.

Receiving Wisdom leads us to the necessity of discernment, the process of making wise judgments. The etymology of "discernment" derives from separation and sifting. It is the inner experience of panning for gold, placing a mass of ore in a solution and agitating it until the gold is extracted. There is nothing "bad" about the non-gold ore, but we must learn to distinguish what is useful for what purpose. Knowledge is like undifferentiated ore. Wisdom is what helps us know what to do with it.

St. Ignatius of Loyola developed a practice he called the "discernment of spirits" after a long convalescence, during which he observed the "movements in the soul."[43] His practice was to observe the thoughts that corresponded to pleasant, elevating feelings, and those thoughts that caused disruptive and discordant feelings. From this observation, he developed a framework by which to evaluate the influence of these "spirits" upon the soul.[44] Elevating spirits came from the Christian god and good angels, whereas the disruptive and discordant feelings came from evil angels. By contemplating the action of spirits upon the soul, discernment leads those following Ignatius to choose to follow the guidance of his god and disregard that of the adversary.

Paganism and polytheism need their own discernment practices. Anomalous Thracian identifies the "three Ds" that are integral to discernment: distinctions, differentiation, and definitions.[44] These "Ds" matter, as we do not have simple dualism for the categorization of possible influences and sources of information. Our categories do not fall neatly into "all good" and "all bad." We might wonder if our trance visions, dreams, teachings, insights, or spontaneous intuitions come from God Soul, a deity, an ancestor, a Spirit of Place, a fae being, an alien, or our personal hopes and fears. We might be thrown into confusion when one friend claims their god wants animal sacrifice while another claims the same god abhors the offerings of blood and flesh. We might wonder whom to believe, how to measure the truth of these, what is real.

These questions are not mere navel-gazing, though they might matter more to humans than to the gods. At the heart of these questions for spiritual seekers and practitioners are thorny political and sectarian issues with which we wrestle. Certain radical feminist goddess worshippers assert that

---

43. Saint Ignatius of Loyola, "Rules for Perceiving and Knowing in some Manner the Different Movements which are Caused in the Soul," *The Spiritual Exercises of St. Ignatius of Loyola*, translated by Elder Mullan, 1914, http://http://www.sacred-texts.com/chr/seil/.
45. Anomalous Thracian, "The Letter 'D'," *Thracian Exodus*, 12 July 2015, https://thracianexodus.wordpress.com/2015/07/12/the-letter-d/: "Discernment requires the ability to recognize distinctions, which call for the active differentiation between some things from other things, which in turn relies on the knowledge or ability to seek the knowledge of the specific definitions related to those and other things."
"

their goddess does not recognize trans women as women. Some white reconstructionist and so-called "traditionalist" communities claim that their gods do not recognize people of color as legitimate worshippers. I am a white, cisgender gay man of Irish, German, and Italian ancestry, yet none of the deities associated with those pagan cultures take interest in me in the way that the Kemetic deities have. There are African-American practitioners of Kemetic traditions and modern-day Egyptians who would argue that their gods would have no reason to interact with a white person. Yet if I believe the gods are real and have their own agency, I cannot pretend that my experiences are not happening.

For much of my life I have been beset by doubts, even as I feel a deep yearning for connection to the divine. I have experienced powerful confirmations of my personal work and yet I encounter people who radiate such charisma and certainty that it leaves me reeling for days, worrying I am simply a fraud. When faced with apparent certainty, I feel confusion and fascination. What would it be like to be so certain of one's experience and beliefs?

Experiences are simply what they are; it is the meaning we attach to the experience that leads us to take particular actions. Those actions generate outcomes that either confirm or complicate our sense of meaning. For example: I ask a diviner to do a reading on a job offer. The diviner lays out an arrangement of Tarot cards (experience) and then offers an interpretation (meaning) that the job would cause me suffering. I listen to this reading (experience) and feel frustration and disappointment because I want this job, and decide that this diviner doesn't know what they're doing (meaning). So I take the job (action), and within a month find myself overwhelmed and miserable (outcome), leading me to reconsider that the diviner was accurate (meaning).

Discernment occurs in the realm of meaning. We do not need to tear apart our experience so much as sift through our filters to help us choose effective action. These filters include:

- **Personal Psychology:** What does this experience mean to me? What do I want it to mean? What do I fear it means? How does my history shape my experience of the present? Am I repeating a pattern that often causes me suffering? Does this gnosis make me too comfortable or too uncomfortable? Does it neatly fit my biases and preconceptions?
- **Cultural Context:** Does this experience seem to cohere with or push against the cultures I inhabit? Will following my understanding of my experience result in a violation of cultural boundaries, either my own or another's?
- **Historical/Political Context:** If I am working with information about Beings who have been known at other historical eras, what did humans in those eras think about the Beings? What do we know about their practices? Does my gnosis align with or contradict theirs?[46] What are my modern-day biases? How might they inform or deform the information I receive?
- **Community:** What do my peers and elders think? What information have they received? What questions or concerns do they raise when I share this information?

Victor Anderson advised, when encountering a god or spirit, to "turn on your porch light and see who's there!" When I have conversations with Beings that give me pause, I stop to align with my God Soul and then ask the being to identify itself or reveal its true nature. Those of us who have tools of sovereignty, like wands and blades, could draw upon these to demand this information.

I use "demand" intentionally. Generally I do not demand things of gods and spirits, but I feel it appropriate in this circumstance. When a human stranger knocks on my door and says they want to come in and work on my plumbing, I have a right to demand they verify they are who they purport to be before offering hospitality. We are not obligated to acquiesce to any random spirit.

---

46. A note pointing out that contradiction does not automatically mean invalidation. Much of what Crowley and the Golden Dawn understood about Egyptology at the time has not borne out with continued scholarship. The gods may change over time, and there may be more to learn than is currently understood.

Another practice of discernment I use draws upon my voice and body. You might try doing this practice with the communication medium that is most natural to you. This is particularly useful when trying to discern a course of action about which you feel confused.

- Explore the situation and your inner conflicts around it.
- Identify potential action statements. You are not committing to any of these at this time, so write out as many possibilities as you wish. It helps to frame these actions as choices, like: "I will..." "I won't..." "I choose to..." "I choose not to..."[47]
- Start with one statement that resonates strongly with you.
- Breathe into your body and open your senses.
- Speak the statement and notice how it feels in your body.
- Speak the opposite of the statement and notice how it feels in your body.
- Continue with as many statements as you wish.

The body's responses help us to validate our own inner longings and separate out from the "shoulds" of the ego. It guides us toward our authentic boundaries. Instinctive and emotional wisdom comes through this practice. When I do this practice, I choose to follow the statements that cause my body to feel lighter, stronger, more energized, and avoid the statements that cause my body to feel heavy, stressed, and upset.

The vibratory movement from Water through Passion to Wisdom is the journey from raw elemental force through human consciousness into that which is beyond the personal. Studying the patterns and essence of Water deepens our understanding of Passion and increases Wisdom. Following rote practices "because you must" or holding rigid beliefs "because they are right" fall out of the flow of Wisdom. Wisdom has to move. Water's greatest Wisdom is its fluidity. It takes whatever form it must. It erodes obstacles while simultaneously flowing around them. Water seeks balance and will flow to where it is lacking, or drain from where it is excessive. The flow of Wisdom brings us intuitively to wholeness.

---

47. Reclaiming teachers Dawn Isidora and Jennifer Byers first taught me this practice of using active choice language.

FIRE, PRIDE, LAW: LIVES WITH WORTH

Auset fled to the marshes after escaping Set's imprisonment, attended by seven guardian scorpions provided by Djehuti. Disguised as a beggar, Auset traveled. When she came upon a town, Auset found the house of a rich woman to ask for food and a place to sleep. The rich woman slammed the door in Auset's face, not knowing who she was. The goddess continued searching for shelter and found a poor fisherwoman who welcomed her, gave her food, and gave her a place to sleep.

As Auset slept, the scorpions shared their anger over the rich woman's refusal. They combined their venom into the stinger of the leader, who went to avenge their mistress. The scorpion snuck into the wealthy woman's house and came upon her infant child first. With all its rage, the scorpion stung the infant and fled.

The next morning, the rich woman found her child suffering and ran into the town crying out for help. When Auset saw the woman and her child, her heart softened and she realized what had occurred. Auset offered her skill and called out each scorpion's name to withdraw the venom from the child's body. The rich woman was overcome with regret, now recognizing Auset for who she was, and offered her wealth to the goddess. Auset asked instead that the rich woman give a portion of her wealth to the generous fisherwoman.

Try this: imagine a hand grabbing the crown of your head, pulling upward such that your neck, shoulders, and pelvis align. Let your spine left from your hips, and feel your seat through the bones in your butt. Notice how that influences the flow and sensation of life force. Notice the shift in your energy, your thoughts, your perspective. Invoke Pride.

Pride is your claim to membership in this world. Simply by being, you have a right to air, space, and food. This claim exists whether or not you "earn" it. Take up the space you need, from your feet to the top of your head. Own your wants and needs. Pride is a candle, lighting you from within.

Pride is being right-sized and in right-relationship, knowing our gifts and limitations, recognizing when I have something to offer, and stepping back when it is time for others to shine. I have capacities I want to develop, and can develop, with disciplined effort. I have blind spots to accommodate and work on improving.

Pride is recognizing my "enough-ness." Through Pride I make contact with my innate worth and value and sense that I am enough for this life. Sometimes I demonstrate Pride by saying, "I will not help you, but I could help you find someone who can." We do not have to be all things for all people. We're not supposed to solve all of the problems of the world by ourselves. Each of us has our piece of the answer.

Fire and Pride

The etymology of the word "enthusiasm" connects to Greek roots that suggest "divinely inspired" or "possessed by a god."[48] Our sacred source longs to emerge in the manifest realm as we may long to be connected to it. That divine inspiration enters through Sex and connects to ground at Pride, where we must tend its energy. Like fire, Pride needs steady and dedicated tending. Too little attention, and it dies out. Too much, and it spirals out of control. This sacred fire is our birthright and yet not wholly "ours."

---

48. Thanks to etymonline.com.

The iron of our blood was emitted from the last stage of a star's nuclear fusion. Our bodies are made of carbon from the plants or animals we eat. We feed fire with dead plant matter, leaving behind ash that feeds new plant and animal life. Fire gives light and warmth, and it consumes. To live is to consume, to affect our environment, to take in what we need and release what we do not. We breathe in the waste oxygen of trees, and exhale the carbon dioxide these trees need.

All of this pertains to Pride, our basic sense of aliveness. That fundamental knowledge that I am worth the materials I consume. For us, the matter of our living bodies is not "waste," it is necessity. What we produce as "waste" is necessity for other forms of life. We are capable of a vibrant pattern of exchange which contributes to a functioning ecosystem.

One of the greatest injuries we've done to our cultures and planet is creating the concept of "garbage," materials that lack value and can only be "thrown away." We convince ourselves that there is an "away" where we won't have to worry about these things anymore, but then they show up in the bodies of dead animals and vanishing species. We do this with the people we deem valueless as a society—disrupting their homeless encampments, throwing them into prisons, or harassing them out of our communities. As a globally-conscious species we now must wrestle with the reality that there is no "away." Garbage continues to exist and toxifies our world.

It is time to look at ways to keep our waste in the flow that supports our planet's ecosystems. It's time to stop labeling people as "garbage" and throwing them away. And we may start within. What in you feels unworthy, without value? What in you do you cast aside, put in jail, keep hidden? What in you feels like waste? What if all of this could serve your higher purpose, your Great Work? What if you could stop being at war with yourself and stand tall?

The following exercise can help you to connect to your sense of Pride today, your basic sense of aliveness:

Breathe into the sounds of your environment and exhale, imagining your attention to those sounds rippling away from you in a wave, leaving stillness at the center. Breathe into your thoughts and exhale, imagining your attention to thoughts rippling away in a wave, leaving stillness at the center. Breathe into your feelings and exhale, imagining your attention to those feelings rippling away in a wave, leaving stillness at the center. Breathe into your bodily sensations and exhale, imagining your attention to those sensations rippling away in a wave, leaving stillness at the center.

From this still place, notice the feeling of energy and aliveness in your body. This may feel subtle at first, or hard to understand. Focus on a part of your body, like your hand. What energy in the hand signifies aliveness? How does aliveness feel inside of you?

Stay with the feeling of aliveness. Notice any energetic blocks, stuck feelings, or problematic thoughts. Notice how your aliveness responds to these. Then acknowledge the block, feeling, or thought, and invite it to be present with you in attending to the sense of aliveness. Notice the overall flow and quality of energy, of aliveness.

Ask this aliveness to give you an image that symbolizes it. This image might appear as a visualization, a felt sense in your body, an emotion, a word or phrase. If nothing comes up, stay with the felt sense of the aliveness in your body. Ask the image or felt sense to help you understand what feeds your sense of Pride. Attend to any response that happens. Ask the image to help you understand what blocks or undermines Pride. Attend to any response that happens.

Thank yourself for showing up, and your sense of aliveness and Pride. On four deep breaths, call your attention back through your body, heart, mind, and into your environment. Write down your observations and any messages you received. Do what helps you to ground.

Pride Centering Self: The Still, Expansive Core

We have many unique, often conflicting parts of self. C. G. Jung described these as "complexes," sensitive clusters of emotional energy that have autonomous wants and fears. Roberto Assagioli spoke of "subpersonalities," suggesting that these parts have unique worldviews and experiences. I can label "parts" that seem to be constellations of experiences organized around a particular emotional energy or story: the part that feels hopeless, the part that feels "everyone's against me," and so forth. Dr. Richard Schwartz suggests that these parts become mired in conflict and work at cross-purposes when the natural leader and center of the system is absent, what he calls "Self."[49]

What goes awry, according to Schwartz, is that we experience overwhelming problems at points in our early childhood development. Other parts of us take control and hide the "Self" away for safekeeping. When the crisis passes, if we are unsupported or in unstable situations, our protective and wounded parts may no longer trust "Self" to resume leadership. Without its unconditionally loving presence, unbalanced parts vie for dominance. A part that believes "to be safe everything has to be perfect" may then suppress or attack other parts that feel imperfect or threatening. This part feels under near-constant assault since nothing is perfect. When "Self" is present, however, this part can let go of the burden of control and focus on its natural gifts, like being detail-oriented or having a strong moral sense.

In the esoteric psychology explored in this book, our alignment with God Soul is analogous to being in Schwartz's state of "Self." God Soul is a soft, nonjudgmental, loving awareness that feels like "me" and yet not "me." When centered and aligned, I am better able to recognize all of my parts, attend to them, and then synthesize these disparate wants and needs into an action that satisfies the whole personality.

At times I've been fused with my feelings of inadequacy, and avoided connection with God Soul, fearing it would send a thundering message that I am worthless and wasting my life. When I connect, however, I feel an almost incomprehensible affection. God Soul loves every part of me. God Soul *chooses* every part of me. God Soul expresses near-infinite forbearance. Aligned, those parts of me which seemed like flaws reveal purpose and

---

49. Richard C. Schwartz, *Internal Family Systems Therapy* (New York: Guilford Press, 1995).

needs that my conscious mind did not understand. When I love myself, I stop wasting energy and I do the thing I want to do. When I love myself, I listen to my dislikes and I do not do the thing I do not want to do.

Dropping my center of my consciousness into my physical center supports connection to God Soul. Much of the time my "awareness" seems to live in my head. Years of work helped to expand it more into my heart and body, but the default goes right back up there. My still center dwells in my belly, around my navel and pelvis. Anchoring awareness there and expanding to take in my whole experience helps me be in a holistic experience. Thoughts continue to happen but they no longer feel like the most priority experience. They are information, like the sensations of my body.

When we enter these states of being fully present, we almost instinctively move toward healing and integrity. The trick is that the "I am" is being with all of my parts and not taking sides. Often the ego thinks it needs to pick certain parts that are winners and ignore the rest, which is particularly challenging when parts want mutually exclusive things, and it's unclear which one is "right."

When I started seeing a Jungian therapist, I told him I wanted to work on my indecisiveness. He went to the dictionary, one of his favorite interventions, and found the definition of "decision." Of particular interest to him were its Latin roots, *de* (off) and *caedere* (to cut). To decide, he suggested, meant to cut away a part of myself—the part does not get included in the decision. Instead, he worked with me to listen to these conflicting parts of self and make a "choice" that includes the influence of each. All of this required entering into that state of centered, compassionate presence that is able to listen to the needs and fears of each part with equanimity.

This idea scares some folks. They point to parts of themselves that seem monstrous or toxic, that want to engage in destructive behaviors. Why should these get a vote? For several reasons:

- Problematic parts of self contain deeply buried wants and needs. Because of this, these parts tend to get their due whether we listen or not.

- As we uncover these buried wants and needs and include them, the parts no longer need to be so monstrous and destructive to get our attention.
- Listening to these parts does not mean giving them total control over our choices. We tend to be safer because they are included in a larger inner consensus process. One part wants to start abusing drugs again, but other parts that value sobriety and stability also have a say. This helps us hold their acting-out in check

Early in development, the animal soul—Sticky One, or Fetch—tries out strategies to get its needs met, such as resistance, placating, charming, tantruming, and so forth. The rational soul— Shining Body, or Talker—learns from our caregivers how to manage these emotional needs—redirecting them, shutting them down, indulging them, shaming them, or other strategies. One strategy is for Shining Body to simply refuse to listen to Sticky One, believing their needs to be wholly dangerous or ridiculous. Sticky One may override Shining Body through explosive acting out, unconscious behaviors, and emotional upheaval.

This relationship between soul parts keeps either from fully expressing their potential in harmony. In Feri tradition, it is said that the God Soul speaks directly to Sticky One—so if Shining Body and Sticky One are in dysfunctional relationship, we are going to struggle to express our divinity. Even "successful" dysfunctional patterns validated by society—like overwork, excessive exercise, over-eating—are a violence to the Self, imprisoning tender and harder to love parts.

When our parts are able to see value in each other, the energy we spent managing inner conflict is available for creation. Shining Body helps Sticky One gets its needs met in a time and manner that maximizes benefit and minimizes harm, while Sticky One gathers and holds life force.

The following is a meditation to help you deepen your connection and alignment with your divinity, God Soul:

Find a comfortable posture. Slow your breathing down. Connect with your body. Notice the places of ease and tension, discomfort and relaxation. Notice the feeling of your body connected to the ground. Invite your attention even more deeply into this physical space, into your body.

Notice the part of you that is aware of your body. Notice how this awareness is connected yet separate, able to hold the experience of your body and in some deep way apart from it. Breathe into this awareness, and as you breathe out, relax its connection to your physical body.

Let your awareness rise up into your heart. Notice your emotions, and notice Sticky One around your body. Notice the energies and feelings at play. Invite your attention deeply into this part of you.

Notice again that your awareness is connected yet separate, able to hold the experience of your emotions but remain apart from it in some deep way. Breathe into this awareness, and as you breathe out, relax its connection to your heart.

Let your awareness rise up into your mind. Notice your thoughts, and the energy of Shining Body surrounding you in an oval that extends several inches out from your body. Notice how Shining Body gives and receives information. Notice the movement of your thoughts. Invite your attention deeply into this part of you.

Notice again that your awareness is connected yet separate, able to hold the experience of your mind but remain apart from it in some deep way. Breathe into this awareness, and as you breathe out, relax its connection to your mind.

Let your awareness rise up into your divinity, the sphere above your head known as God Soul. Imagine your awareness expanding into God Soul. Be with whatever information arises.

After a long pause, bring that awareness back into your mind, still connected to God Soul. Notice how Shining Body and your thoughts respond to this awareness. Bring that awareness back into Sticky One, which enfolds your body and extends outward about an inch or two. Notice how your feelings and energy respond to this awareness. Bring this awareness to the still center at your core, and invite it to expand out, encompassing your body and all of your parts.

Take some time to journal this experience, taking note of any images, patterns, or strong feelings you encountered.

Pride Infused with Sex: Shame and Worthiness

Pride is where Sex energy anchors in the manifest world. Because of Sex, I exist. I need no other justification for my life. I have innate worth and value, as does every other life form and spirit. When I hold this truth, I feel joyful and every part of me seems to also have worth and value.

More often, we encounter messages that seem to oppose this idea. Carl Rogers called these "conditions of worth" that arise from the measured distribution of love and affection based on what and who others believe I should be. "You are worthy *if*..." We might begin to internalize these conditions before we understand speech. Children are both dependent and highly attuned to fluctuations in their caregivers' moods and affection; they begin to shape themselves in relation to their caregivers' spoken and unspoken needs and expectations. Children learn what strategies get attention consistently, establishing the nascent personality patterns that protect the vulnerable soul from abandonment.

Children gravitate to positive attention but learn to live with whatever they get. Caregivers who are inconsistent, negligent, or abusive parents imprint deep and toxic patterns. A consistently critical parent instills in the child both the expectation of perfection and the deep hopelessness that nothing they ever do is enough. With abusive parents, the child might internalize the parent's abusive statements and behaviors and turn the behavior against self. They may react explosively, as adults, to external situations that remind them of the abuse, but their reactions might resemble the abuse of their parents. There is a gap between the inner experience and the outer perception.[50]

Sticky One seeks what is life-giving, fun, joyful, animating. Sticky One delights in sensation and being here, knows its birthright instinctively.

---

50. As an aside, there is a popular belief that those who suffer abuse or molestation grow up to become abusers. Much depends on how the abused child is held or not held in the wake of the abuse, how frequently the abuse happened, and what inner and outer resources are available to them before and after the assault.

When Pride is absent, or the capacity for Pride severely damaged through messages imprinted in upbringing, the Rusted point of Shame emerges.[51] Shame is a vortex of pain and despair—to put it gently. Shame says I shouldn't want or need anything, and certainly shouldn't get those wants and needs met, because "I" am bad and whatever "I" want is bad. Shame whispers that there is a core of rottenness inside that can never be seen or else I'll be exiled. Shame whispers that there is essentially something broken about me. Shame says that I am alone in the world with my problems. Shame isolates, humiliates, abases.

In the story of Auset and the Scorpions, the goddess humbled herself to go into hiding, but still had the dignity to approach another and ask for what she needed.[52] The wealthy woman's response, however, was deeply shaming. This shame plunged through Auset, drawing out the venomous response of her scorpions. When the consequences of this unconscious transmission of shame came to light, both Auset and the rich woman experienced healthy guilt: that ability to recognize, "I am not bad, but I did something that needs to be rectified." Both took responsibility for the harm and made amends.

While healthy guilt leads us back into integrity, it is difficult to think of a healthy purpose to shame. Those who advocate Shame note its usefulness for social control. They argue that shaming is necessary to punish certain people and behaviors. In some Christian teachings, shame humbles us to understanding how we affect others.

My observation is that shaming tends to keep us stuck in toxic patterns. If I am bad and worthless, then why make any effort to care for myself through self-improvement? Shame becomes another emotional upset to manage, often with the very behavior I feel shame about. The way we experience and practice Shame today is effective for social control, ineffective at stopping harmful behaviors, and venomous to individual liberty and harmonious, beloved community.

---

51. "Guilt" and "Shame" are often used interchangeably. I like the distinction that Brené Brown utilizes in her book *The Gifts of Imperfection*: Guilt says, "I did something wrong." Shame says, "I am bad."

52. Auset and the Scorpions would be a great band name.

In a state of Shame, I am flooded with painful emotions and overwhelmed by thoughts about my badness. One shaming thought leads to the next, spiraling into an endless vortex. Because this experience is so painful, most of us who are shame-sensitive will react protectively against the experience. Some of us get angry and accuse the other person, anything to deflect from the shaming issue. Another strategy is to over-apologize and self-punish as a way of getting the other person to stop holding us accountable and instead make us feel better. Or someone might withdraw altogether, thinking it's best to disappear and no longer bother anyone.

Not only is this awful for the person feeling the shame, it undermines justice in relationship and community. The shamed person does not take responsibility for their behavior. These outbursts instead punish the person who brought up the problem. Energy goes toward tending, numbing, and alleviating shame and not toward rectification. Surrounding family and community grow wary of approaching the topic again, even if the problematic behavior continues, because they do not want to endure another storm. When the problem continues, however, resentments accumulate and those affected must either withdraw from the person in Shame or act out in their own problematic ways.

My wants and needs don't go away simply because Shame says they're bad. Instead Shame makes me more likely to meet those needs in indirect, sneaky, and disrespectful ways. If I feel intense shame about my sexual wants and needs, then I will feel uncomfortable asking for them. I might tend toward deceptive and coercive strategies to get those needs met, even unconsciously. Shame guides me to suffer resentfully in a relationship that doesn't work, or let my physical needs go unmet because asking for more money or for help is "selfish." Some will push away offers of help because their shame is so deep. Even worse is when this kind of shame is valorized as heroic individualism.

Money is another topic that can put us in Shame, arising from the internalization of plutocratic values.[53] Capitalism values certain forms of labor

---

53. Credit to T. Thorn Coyle for introducing me to the idea of "internalized plutocracy."

more highly than others. Plutocracy says that people who do higher-waged labor are of greater value than those who do lower-waged labor. That is bullshit. Pride is not dependent upon income. If your wages are not enough to meet your needs, that is a failure of the system to distribute resources equitably. There are things we can do as individuals within Capitalism to try to get our needs met and increase our income, but again that does not have anything to do with innate worthiness. I've gone from working in a corporate job making a living wage to working as a gas station clerk for minimum wage within a year due to a recession, and I was the same person. What changed was the work, what I was paid, and how others saw me. Working in a service or low-wage job is itself tolerable, but the passive and overt shaming that comes from customers who see you as an acceptable target for all their daily frustrations and disempowerment is a constant assault on one's Pride.

As a therapist, I've noticed that one of the trickiest problems is when people come in wanting to be "fixed." They have been struggling for a long time, and they want to have hope and want to believe I can help them. The problem is, when someone says they are "broken" and need to be "fixed," that is often Shame speaking. I want to offer hope without agreeing with Shame's messages. Every effort to "fix" only goes so far when we fail to unseat the hidden sovereignty of Shame.

An antidote to Shame is calling in a sense of one's innate worthiness, or the Iron energy of Pride. The following ritual is one tool that could help you with this work:

Create sacred space. Call in any allies you need. Gather your tools of sovereignty, such as your wand or blade. Breathe in Sex energy. Fill your body with Sex. Fill your Sticky One with Sex. Fill your Shining Body with Sex. When you sense you are saturated with life force, breathe up and align with your God Soul. Feel the energy of God Soul sinking into your scalp, through your head and throat, through your heart, through your belly, connecting with your still center. Feel life force arising from your still center, circling around this line like a spiraling serpent, connecting with your God Soul.

Pick up your wand, scepter, or other tool of sovereignty. Breathe life force into this as well. In this space, your words are power.

Begin to name your worthiness. You might start by naming parts of yourself in which you feel pride and worth. "My Sex is worthy." Let yourself be spontaneous with this, saying whatever comes to mind without censoring. If you cannot sense anything worthy about you, try saying something like, "I am willing to know the worthiness of my Sex." Continue with this process, beginning to name parts of yourself that feel harder to name as worthy. Name your wants and needs. Name your suffering and limitations. Name your divinity and your humanity.

If you find this process inhibited by thoughts or feelings of Shame, pause. Name these thoughts and feelings out loud and, with all the sovereignty you possess, demand that they support this working or step aside. Return to the work.

When you feel complete, take a moment to dwell within the feeling of worthiness and Pride. Breathe this energy to your God Soul. If you'd like to do a spell or divination to honor or deepen this work, do so now. Otherwise, thank yourself and the allies who have helped you, and close the ritual.

PRIDE SUPPORTING POWER: AUTHORITY AND ARROGANCE

The Reclaiming tradition of witchcraft's *Principles of Unity* states "our ultimate spiritual authority is within."[54] When I took this on as a truth, it transformed my relationship to teachers, leaders, community, and partners.

What does spiritual authority mean? In my practice, the God Soul is a unique point of connection to God Hirself, and the source of inner spiritual authority. It is the part of our soul that is eldest, most connected with the fullness of experience, eternal, and possessing the wisdom of many lifetimes and incarnations. We each have access to this personal divinity, but many of us feel cut off from it at various points in life.

I believe we discover our authority through seeing it expressed by the people we admire. As adults, our relationship to people with authority tells us a lot about how we relate to inner authority. Do you seek out people to

---

54. Available at http://www.reclaiming.org/about/directions/unity.html.

whom you can submit your will, to always be an inferior? Do you rail against and try to tear down anyone who claims any kind of authority, including yourself? Do you avoid anyone who claims to know any kind of truth? Do you feel intimidated by someone? All of these connect to aspects of power and authority that you could claim and possess for yourself.

In my first Reclaiming community, I noticed a pattern of the community elevating people as celebrated priestesses, only to later turn upon and tear them down. We projected our own power and authority onto the priestesses without consciousness. Instead of tearing down our deified image of the priestess and claiming our own power, we tore down the person. Such conflict is a natural part of growing into Power, and very painful to work through for all involved. We had a hell of a time keeping priestesses engaged and not burnt out.

Too often we look to leaders and powerful people and think there's something uniquely special about them that we do not possess. We do not see the hours of work, daring, and failure that person endured to become who they are today. We also might not notice the help given, the opportunities offered, the privileges that person has available to them. No one is born ready to be a bright star, and no one makes it on their own.

What helps me to cultivate inner authority has been finding people who bring up strong reactions in me, and listening thoughtfully. That sense of "I admire this person. They offer something I want to learn," is the nascent voice of inner authority. To be sure, we are surrounded daily by people who could teach us more about ourselves as we are. What I speak of here are the people who teach us about who we are *capable of becoming*.

When I first began working with my teacher Thorn, I felt intimidated by her steady presence and piercing gaze. I became stricken by anxiety when standing near her, all my parts of self that wanted validation and feared rejection acted up. During one retreat, I recall signaling that I had something to share. She turned toward me and simply said, "Yes." I fought the urge to shrink under the attention, while admiring the simple presence and confidence expressed in the moment. She demanded nothing of me, simply recognized my desire to speak, and yet I felt very visible.

All of these responses were the barriers to me embodying that energy I saw in her. These feelings screamed out against the attention, seeing their days of running my life unchecked were numbered. After years of study I came to recognize how my mannerisms, speech, and style of writing have taken up some resemblance to hers, and I recognize this is only a step toward Self-possession. I need to stoke the courage to walk my own path, find my own language.

When I became a therapist, I sought out therapists whose energy, presence, and work inspired me, and I attended to them in similar ways. In early phases much of this came from insecurity and a belief I needed to reject myself and be more like the people I respected. With time, anchored more firmly in Pride, I have come to see that I am braiding together my own rope from these different strands.

The process is uneven and risky. At times people I like suggest scary and uncomfortable things, but my body senses the suggestion would help me grow. Other times people I thought I respected have convinced me to do things that left me feeling anxious, pressured, and disgusted, recognizing that I was no longer in integrity.

Possessing inner authority is not about saying, "I know the truth and I don't need anyone else to teach me anything." It is accepting that I am in the best position to know myself, and I will live with the consequences of my choices in ways that others will not. I have a unique story in this life, and others' truth is a part of that story, but I am *its author*. So I can accept there are things I do not know, ask better questions, listen deeply, and weigh what is offered against my inner understanding. The allies in this work are experimentation and curiosity.

When we forget curiosity and become enamored of our authority, we fall into the Gilded point of Arrogance. Arrogance, in the Iron Pentacle, carries many of the toxic qualities ascribed to Pride in Christian traditions: contempt, superiority, indifference to how one affects others, and a tendency to impose one's values and beliefs upon others. A person in Arrogance seems completely insensitive to how others experience them but may be highly sensitive to how they are received.

People in Arrogance often serve as great examples of the saying "when you point a finger at someone, three point back at you." A person in Arrogance could complain for hours about how nobody lets them get a word in edgewise, talking over you even when you try to provide supportive comments, oblivious to the irony. Arrogance burns hot and bright and demands more and more fuel. It escalates opinions and preferences to the level of dogma and comes down hard against contrary facts, arguments, or opinions. Arrogance is an aggressive confidence, constantly pushing one's needs and wants forward and taking more and more energy from others to do so.

I once heard a saying that the Gilded Pentacle is what happens when you wrap gold leaf around the Rusted Pentacle. When I am in Arrogance and someone calls me out on it, it is easy to drop deeply into Shame. Once in Shame, I feel that Arrogance was the thinnest layer of ice above a deep and cold lake. This suggests that being fixed in Arrogance is a mode of perpetual avoidance, unable to admit flaws to keep at abeyance the intolerable pain of Shame.

Arrogance is like one polarity of a magnet, drawing out others' shame-sensitivity. People in Arrogance are quite capable of disorienting, harming, and undermining the confidence of those who oppose them. When others feel their vulnerability rising, one response is expressing combative, hostile energy, eliciting a stronger need to defend and repel the hostile external feedback through contempt and disrespect on each side. Others attracted by Arrogance may express fawning, deferential energy, people who project their authority upon the person in Arrogance in the hopes of having it validated.

In Arrogance, one's inner authority is inflated. Those in this state make declarations that smack of "one-true-way-ism." They may have a great deal of experience and research to support their claims; the tell is their unwillingness to entertain alternate views and acknowledge limits to their insight. This is particularly tricky in spaces that strongly value equality or social justice norms, for the person in Arrogance twists these norms to be a shield against criticism or a weapon to bully others.

If authority begins and ends within us, if all authority emerges from relationship with God Soul, then ultimately our work is to call in authority from others. Effective teachers, priestesses and priests, therapists, and leaders hold and reflect that authority until we're ready to take it back. People who are not healthy in relationship to their parts are vulnerable to internalizing the projected authority and star power, believing it is actually theirs or given by the gods. That fosters dependency between both leader and follower, an endless circle of seeking, giving, or denying validation that depletes both even as it seems to bolster the ego. Left unchecked, this dynamic leads to devastating communal and personal consequences. We are not exempt from the dangers and flaws of human groups simply because we are witches, polytheists, priests, activists, anarchists, or what have you. To be identified with our communal or mythic roles is to risk a dangerous inflation. We must remember our true Selves and not confuse them with the roles we play.

The following exercise supports us in claiming inner authority and healthy Pride. The goddess Auset, or Isis, blesses this work. Her name means "throne." She is the seat of power and the voice that makes decree. She may help you find these within yourself, that you may become Self-ruled. If you have a relationship with her, you might ask for her assistance in this. Sandalwood incense is an appropriate offering, and lapis lazuli a key to her presence. Otherwise you might ask for help from a deity related to sovereignty and rulership with which you have connection.

Take four deep breaths: one into your body, one into your Sticky One, one into Shining Body, and the fourth into all of your parts. Breathe the energy up to your God Soul and open to the cord of connection sinking through your skull, your neck, your chest, into the still place at the center of yourself.

Breathe into this still place, touching center, and breathe out, connecting to your edges. Ask the question, "Where is the seat of my authority?" Drop it into your center and let it resonate out through all of your parts. Wait for an answer to come. If parts of you say you have no authority, acknowledge those and invite them to help you find it. If they refuse, then tell them to step aside.

When you have an answer, or feel you have spent enough time sitting with the question, then imagine all those people, traditions, and institutions that to you have authority. Gather in that authority to yourself. Gather it to feed your own inner authority, whether it is currently known or not.

Now offer gratitude. Offer gratitude to the gods, your teachers, your priests and priestesses, your leaders, those people who have inspired you, those people who seem more knowing than you. Offer gratitude to those who used their authority wisely and well and helped you. Continue offering gratitude to those who misused their authority, who failed out of ignorance or willfulness but still taught you something. Offer gratitude to those who taught you the kind of person you do not want to be. Offer gratitude to yourself for showing up, then and now. Offer gratitude to your inner authority, that still small voice inside.

Return to stillness and sit with what you feel in your soul parts. Breathe the energy back up to God Soul.

Pride Fed by Passion: When Skill Meets Need

As I began writing this, I saw a social media post from my friend, interior designer Seán Kendig: "There's something really wonderful that occurs mentally when you're able to align your skills in such a manner that it allows you to be useful in some way that is needed... I'm not curing cancer, saving the world or saving lives but I will be making a positive contribution in a way that will make difference in someone's day to day life."

Seán's statement speaks to me of the flow of Passion into Pride. He holds his work in right-sized perspective, recognizing the greater context in which his work exists while owning his positive influence. He celebrates the "something really wonderful" that happens when what we love to do meets what we are skilled at doing, and best of all when this meeting has a valued impact on others. As much as we can only do what feels right for us, we are social creatures whose work exists in a context.

It is painful to present Passion-filled work that is poorly received, or received with indifference. It is draining to deliver skilled work that is well-executed and well-received but disconnected from Passion. Being of service or rewarded brings satisfaction, but it demands energy to stay focused on what generates little interest. When I go through phases of doing work that is necessary but devoid of Passion, I look at how the benefits of it support my larger works of Passion. If the energy costs exceed the benefits, it's time to look at options and start planning my exit.

Discovering the need we meet, the niche in which our work flourishes, is Pride work. So too is the work of leaving comfortable places in which we can grow no more. This could look like learning a new skill, taking a long-postponed risk, finding a larger need that my work could meet. A potted plant can only grow so large before it needs to be moved to a bigger container, its roots broken up so they can expand.

We could grow upward and outward, expanding our scope and reach of influence, concern, and effort. This is not universally praised; in small, close-knit communities, such ambition stirs up hostility, feelings of abandonment, and criticism. Struggling communities become very proud and attached to their bright stars and afraid that as the person grows larger, they will forget the needs of their home community. This is a legitimate fear.

We could grow downward and inward, finding new subtleties to explore, new applications of our skills, new forms of service and relationship with community. Perhaps we approach a familiar passion from an unfamiliar direction. After years of direct service, I may start working on advocacy and administration. I may take a class to get a new perspective, or I may step out of theory and try taking a class that engages my body. This means looking at what matters most to me and stepping back from the current way I go about doing it, wondering if there is another path.

In my field, continuing education is a requirement. Going to workshops invigorates me when I am feeling stretched thin and drained. Even if the tools offered do not interest me, I enjoy spending time with colleagues to talk theory and practice. It is the same with spiritual practice. I have a strong daily practice, but the energy of that begins to wane unless I connect with community and open to new ideas, new possibilities, and shared enthusiasm.

Invite the energy of Pride into your body, and notice the posture you want to take. Stand fully as yourself, as you are, with all your skills and passions. What are you? A tool for the gods? A worker of magic? A priest? What does your Pride serve?

Practice walking with Pride. Make a list of your accomplishments and challenges you've overcome. What challenge is before you?

PRIDE EXALTED IN LAW

Maat:
Lady of Judgment, True of Mind,
Mystery of the greater Law.
In You we seek the harmony
of liberation and structure,
fabrication and exchange,
causality and consequence.
Unbind the oppressions of body
And measure our hearts with honor

In Kemetic depictions of the experience after death, when the recently departed enter the Hall of Judgment, Anpu (or Anubis, the jackal-headed god) weighs their hearts against the Feather of Ma'at. Hearts that weigh equal to, or lighter than, the feather belong to those who have lived lives of virtue and worthiness, who are allowed to proceed to the next phase of transformation. Those hearts that are too heavy are fed to the Devourer of Souls, suggesting annihilation or, possibly, re-absorption into the material world.

This seems a straightforward model, an antecedent to Christian models of afterlife judgment. Yet throughout the texts of funerary spells, one sees many opportunities to intervene. Priests recite the spells and make the sacred offerings necessary to facilitate the departed soul's journey through the afterworld. The departed souls, upon entering the Hall of Judgment, may make Negative Confessions and divest themselves of the weight of unrighteousness and unresolved pain.[55]

A scale is a model of relationship. With a pan scale, balance requires that the two weights seek a sustainable position, at times necessitating the adjustment of the beam and the fulcrum. When the weights are equal, balance occurs with the fulcrum at the center of the beam. With unequal weights, the fulcrum needs to be closer to the heavier weight to establish balance. One of Anpu's roles is to prepare the scale of Ma'at, which provides him the opportunity to make the measurement favorable or unfavorable to the soul using this principle.

These images associated with Ma'at suggest that living in integrity results in a heart that is feather-light, joyful. Ma'at seems the appropriate deity for Law as she evokes greater social and cosmic order, the innate rhythms and laws of the universe, as well as those social laws which foster justly working societies. Instead of a mechanistic universe that grinds eternally in empty patterns, Ma'at is the active, living, dynamic Law that sustains existence, life, and the rhythms of God Hirself.

Pride brings us to Law. When we are honest with ourselves and accept who we are, setting aside facile judgments of "good" and "bad" qualities, we live with integrity. I ask for what I want and pay what you deserve. My needs are worthy of being met, and yet no one is obligated to meet them. We need the willing, uncoerced cooperation of others.

Law steps beyond morality and into consequential ethics, in which one's behavior is judged by its impact. Our behavior is not ruled by threat and authoritarian pronouncement; instead we accept responsibility for the outcome of our choices. You can do whatever you like, but you cannot escape the consequences of your choices.

---

55. The "negative confession" is a performative act, whereupon speaking it makes it so. "I am not deceitful" is one such confession, releasing deceitfulness rather than stating a fact.

In the United States, the current criminal justice systems seems to dehumanize everyone involved—victims, perpetrators, and those who fall into the more messy categories such as "accused but innocent" and "victimized but not innocent." The label of "innocence" is applied unevenly along lines of race and gender; a twenty year-old white male prosecuted for sexual assault was described as "baby-faced," "All-American," and someone who does not "look like a rapist."[56] Meanwhile, an unarmed eighteen year old Black male was shot to death by a police officer after jaywalking, and one news writer made a point to say he was "no angel."[57]

A facile morality suggests that people who commit crimes are a distinct group: "bad people," who hurt "good people" and need to be separated out from the "good people" by any means necessary. Eugenicists love to imagine genetic, racialized markers of criminality that could anticipate when a fetus will turn out to be a "bad person." Others simply endorse or tacitly permit the incarceration, harassment, disenfranchisement, or extrajudicial killing of "bad people," a reassuringly vague category that at times extends to include people who were pulled over for a busted taillight and shot for no apparent reason other than their race.

Operating from a fear-based notion of "law and order," the police must behave with brittle rigidity. In the United States, people can be arrested by the police with the sole charge being "resisting arrest," meaning the person literally committed no crime until the police officer decided to arrest them.

People in the United States say that the accused are "innocent until proven guilty," but when guilty they are appropriately sentenced for their crimes, do their time in prison, and then try to live a rehabilitated life. In practice, what happens is that the public collectively decides upon the innocence or guilt of an accused victim or perpetrator based on media reports, and mark them with that for eternity.

---

56. Michael Miller, "All-American swimmer found guilty of sexually assaulting unconscious woman on Stanford campus," *The Washington Post*, 31 March 2016, https://www.washingtonpost.com/news/morning-mix/wp/2016/03/31/all-american-swimmer-found-guilty-of-sexually-assaulting-unconscious-woman-on-stanford-campus/.
57. John Eligon, "Michael Brown Spent Last Weeks Grappling with Problems and Promise," *The New York Times*, 24 August 2014, https://www.nytimes.com/2014/08/25/us/michael-brown-spent-last-weeks-grappling-with-lifes-mysteries.html.

According to the Rape, Abuse, and Incest National Network, approximately 344 out of every 1,000 rapes in the United States are reported to police, and of those only 6 result in the perpetrator's incarceration.[58] Those who have been sexually assaulted—overwhelmingly but not exclusively cisgender and transgender women—frequently experience reluctance to turn to the police. Some reasons for this include realistic concerns of not being believed, being treated with disrespect, and being vilified—in sexual crimes, the media and justice systems communicate that the alleged victim's alleged virtuousness somehow is relevant to whether the crime occurred. These messages slip in throughout the process of reporting and prosecuting the crime, compounding the survivor's trauma.

On the other side, those perpetrators who are prosecuted, do their time, and succeed at meeting all that is required of them are released to nearly impossible lives as registered sex offenders. They struggle to find housing due to both the legal limits on where they can live and the enormous stigma they carry, leading to people unwilling to house or employ them.

So both victim and perpetrator are harmed by an antagonistic, overstuffed judicial system that serves as an indirect revenue generator for the government. The poorest become entrapped in cycles of debt and incarceration when they cannot afford to pay their ever-mounting fees. In some states, prisons return people to the street with few supports, little money, nowhere to live, and a criminal record. Released inmates may have had no opportunity to develop skills or financial resources that would improve their lives, and now must live with the stigma of their crime and any trauma endured in prison.

This justice system is not rooted in Pride, and thus Law is oppressive. When we do not begin with an assumption of the inherent dignity and worth of all beings, we give ourselves permission to rank worthiness, to dismiss, to marginalize and throw away.[59] This criminal justice system oper-

---

58. "The Criminal Justice System: Statistics," *RAINN*, https://www.rainn.org/statistics/criminal-justice-system."
59. There is not, to my knowledge, an equivalent of Rusted or Gilded Pentacles relative to the Pearl Pentacle. My notion is that Pearl energy itself becomes oppressive and toxic when Iron is absent

ates from a framework of control and punishment. If you hurt someone, then justice requires you suffer hurt as well.

Restorative models of justice see restitution from another angle: mending the personal, communal, and social harms done by the crime. This practice brings in every person with a stake in the crime to participate, speak their truths, and find a resolution that brings healing to the victims and those affected by the crime. The result brings the offender back into community, restoring balance.

Pride and innate dignity offer a better foundation for workable ethics than "right" and "wrong": while there is nothing "wrong" with pumping gallons upon gallons of toxins into the environment, the mass extinctions and climate change such acts cause lead to geopolitical catastrophe, involving many more persons in the act and its consequences. And certainly those creatures, lakes, and spirits of wind who must endure our toxins have a say and may bring their own complaints against us.

Free market advocates invoke Law as something that would naturally dictate and shape the norms of producers and consumers, an "invisible hand" that ensures the greatest profit and outcomes without government intervention. What we live in today is nothing like the free market Adam Smith envisioned. Corporations do not use their profits to pay for the cleanup or mitigation of damage to the environment caused by their products. They may charge the consumers more, ignore the costs altogether, or solicit government subsidies to clean up their messes. Capitalism cannot exist without government intervention—at minimum to form and sustain corporate structures, protect private property, and now to subsidize through welfare the consequences of not paying workers a living wage.

While paying the full, long-term costs of production, labor, and consumption, we would do well to acknowledge the rights of our natural world. If an ocean has an intrinsic right to maintain its own homeostasis in harmony with human needs, then we as humans would have a responsibility to clean up our messes, to not dump chemicals into the oceans, to not destroy the ecology through overfishing or damaging the coral. We would be responsible for repairing the damage we inevitably cause.

Greater Law brings our shortsightedness into balance. All that we've gained will dissolve as the climate changes and our exhausted ecosystems no longer meet our demand. We cannot argue with this Law. It is not personal. It is not about subjective fairness. These dances of life and death, scarcity and abundance, consumption and decomposition, and the forces of gravity and quantum physics are outer facets of Law, Law within the material dimensions.

Smaller laws come from family, community, culture, and social structures such as the government. In one family, everyone simply behaves as though they "know" that they do not point out to grandma that her memory is slipping. Some of us work ourselves to death because we "know" saying no to extra work will endanger our jobs. I write "know" in quotes because these laws are often subconscious, unnamed, and energetic. They are more in the realms of behavior, action, and automatic instinct. Much of their controlling influence comes from not being named and consciously interrogated. Ruled by such laws, we lack perspective, though we easily see the effects of such laws in others. They are the repetitive, automatic behaviors, exaggerated responses, and community norms.

On a social level, Law is enacted through the confluence of power and language. These laws codify norms and behaviors through language precise enough to capture the desired outcome and vague enough to allow room for growth and interpretation. Coming from the government, they are prescriptive, shaping behavior through incentive and punishment. Such laws are rather blunt interventions that often have a host of unintended consequences.

One very illustrative example comes from China, which has the adage "It is better to hit to kill than hit and injure."[60] Drivers who hit and severely impair a pedestrian in China are responsible for that person's healthcare for the rest of their life, whereas a driver who kills a pedestrian only has to pay

---

60. Geoffrey Sant, "Why drivers in China intentionally kill the pedestrians they hit," *Slate.com*, http://www.slate.com/articles/news_and_politics/foreigners/2015/09/why_drivers_in_china_intentionally_kill_the_pedestrians_they_hit_china_s.html.

for burial expenses. As a result, it is apparently a relatively common practice for drivers who accidentally hit pedestrians to intentionally reverse and hit the pedestrians again to ensure they are dead. This is an example of a well-intentioned law that distorted behavior with severe and unwanted consequences.

Reading this is horrifying, but it is less important to judge China and more important to question how our own State's laws shape our behaviors. The rise of the for-profit prison industry in the United States has generated for-profit prison industry lobbyists, who petition local governments to enact more stringent laws to create more criminal acts to create more criminals to create more demand for for-profit prisons. In the United States, shareholders can sue CEOs for failure to execute their fiduciary duties; which means if a CEO realized their company was acting harmfully, but correcting the behavior damaged the company's profitability, then the CEO could be sued. These legal norms virtually ensure the continuation and deepening of widespread harm. Pride-centered Law centralizes the innate dignity and worthiness of all beings, rather than profit, as the ultimate aim and measure of their effectiveness.

We need both Libra and Scorpio energies. As neighbors on the Zodiac these two signs have tension. Venus-ruled Libra loves making contracts, agreements, and harmonious arrangements that bring relationships into a working balance, but shies away from Scorpio's messier territory of fear, control, lust for power, and the deeper psychological dynamics that drive the group. Scorpio, traditionally considered to be ruled by Mars and now by Pluto, brings forward these dynamics to lay them bare. If we approach these with acceptance, understanding that this is a part of our humanity, and include them in Libran deliberations, our agreements become cleaner and more effective. If we avoid them because they are uncomfortable and messy, they will sabotage our work.

I have sat through many meetings in which we all ostensibly had the opportunity to voice our grievances, only for people with long-held grudges to remain silent on everything that bothers them. Whatever we decided in those meetings failed to take because that energy was withheld, was not included and invested in the group process. We did not excavate the layers of power and privilege that inhibit free conversation. We pretended that we were equal and didn't acknowledge that some voices truly had more influence in the room—our boss had power over our working conditions, and certain coworkers were opinion leaders who poisoned the well with cynicism. A Libran process aspires to a position in which all are equal, and a Scorpionic process recognizes that we are embedded in dynamics of power. Better to put all of our weapons on the table and have an honest negotiation.

The lemniscate or infinity symbol is another symbol that evokes Law as energy exchange. One form of lemniscate Law is the give and take of respiration and photosynthesis. Both animal and plant take what they need and release what they does not, benefiting the other. Some day my body will be compost for more plants, or become food for other animals, and until then I must consume formerly living beings. Nothing is garbage; it is all of use.

Law as movement and exchange gives me an ethical guideline. When I'm stuck and don't know what to do, I wonder what will help the system move? What is backed up or depleted? Clogged systems of energy generates tension that threatens weaker parts of the system. When hostility, anger, or protest erupts, instead of simply putting out the fires, we need to look at the underlying conditions that made fire inevitable.

The journey of Law along the Body of Shu shows paths of integrating one's personal truth into communal laws and norms, versus renouncing external constraint in favor of adhering to the inner Law revealed by God Soul. A person journeying these paths may not take a linear route. They may change course at any time, or attempt to integrate both paths.

THE TAROT SUIT OF WANDS & THE JOURNEY OF LAW

ACE OF WANDS

The Subject is sovereign unto themselves, aligned with deep purpose and drive. There is only one Law, that which emerges from the instincts aligned with God Soul, and the subject acts with autonomy. The Subject troubles the communities they have contact with, who either wish to repel or assimilate.

TWO OF WANDS

The Subject struggles with the basic question of dominance or submission in their relationship to others. They are so aligned with their own raw vitality and Law that they struggle to negotiate and make accommodation. They seek to integrate their beliefs and values into their communities.

The Subject now stands possessing truth and their autonomy, turning away from any obligation other than their own inner Law. Complete unto themself, the Subject possesses the world.

THREE OF WANDS

The Subject resolves the polarity of dominance and submission, creating a new vision to move forward, integrating both personal and communal Laws.

The inner Law calls the subject to remove further from the binding rules of community and family, turning toward a vision of Self-possession. They may fear being wholly alone, cut off from community.

FOUR OF WANDS

The Subject learns to make accord with others. The four Staves represent the form and balance of mutual agreements of behavior, making stability possible. The Subject is able to be in community with others like them.

The Subject finds like-minded people, connecting in joy, autonomy, and mutual agreement aligned with inner Law. The four Staves need not be lashed together. Standing on their own, they form the needed supports.

Circling The Star

Five of Wands

Community brings discord as each person's motivations and desires push against the agreements. The Subject's certainty is put to the test as he must endure the challenge to his guiding beliefs. The community must become flexible enough to accommodate challenge but sturdy enough to stay together.

Followers and friends turn on the subject in the process of claiming their own inner Law. Some try to keep the subject in the known; others wish to tear down the subject's perceived arrogance. The subject endures this, recognizing what must happening and knowing this too is the path of God Soul.

Six of Wands

The conflict of the Five resolves into a new set of agreements. The Subject emerges victorious, having created stability at some sacrifice to the dominance of their own truth. They must make accommodations and compromises to keep peace.

Inspired by the Subject's stand, others come to support and follow the subject. They long to experience the Subject's fire and connection to inner Law and make the Subject their hero.

Seven of Wands

More challenges arise against the Subject's truth and beliefs. The Subject feels beset, trying to maintain what gains they had, losing sight of what mattered in the first place. Everyone has a different criticism and the Subject feels alone in a sea of politics and enemies.

Further enlivened by self-assertion, the Subject begins asserting themselves more consciously and connecting to their own truth. They are willing to stand outside the community's norms to discern what inner Law calls to them.

Eight of Wands

A new balance emerges from the conflict, either a state of war or alignment. Either way the agreements are tenuous and rapidly made, a short-term resolution to a longer-term problem.

The effort of the Nine stimulates a greater change than expected. The subject experiences moments of synchronicity in which it feels as though greater forces are aligning to support their will.

Nine of Wands

The Subject becomes a politician, attempting to harden and defend what peace and structure is gained. Their inner sense of Law is given over to the regulations of community and government. Instead of being an autonomous agent, they are wholly subject and defensive of their subjectivity.

Emboldened, the Subject brings their little fire to the community and begins to challenge the status quo. They point out the injuries caused by the prevailing laws and beliefs, and begin letting go of others' expectations and demands to discover their own deep wants.

Ten of Wands

Beneath the obligations and expectations of others, the Subject walks with burden. They have forgotten their capacity to choose, or they have fully chosen to be of service to the laws and beliefs of others and abdicated Self-authority. They'd rather suffer than cause further discord and invite more conflict. They feel the chronic traumas of oppression. When they feel the low burn of their fire, however, a part of them dreams of the possibility of becoming Self-possessed. They long to throw down their burdens and oppressions and rise.

We are not made to be rigid and fixed; instead we dance in relationship between the inner and outer worlds. We act. The world responds. We listen. We act. The world responds. We listen. At times we must make large adjustments to correct for the feedback we're receiving. Other times the adjustments are subtle, as simple as taking a deep breath and giving space to anger. Flexible, adaptive, resilient: Law, enlivened by Fire, anchored in Pride.

Earth, Power, Liberty: Stillness and Strength

Set stands at the bow of the Barque of a Million Years, weapon drawn. Behind him sits Re, vulnerable, restored to his infancy by the journey through the Houses of Night. The final House is all darkness, silence, and still water, but Set senses the threat lurking below. Serpentine coils rise and upset the barque. The water grows more turbulent until the serpent ~~Apep~~ raises his horny skull. ~~Apep~~'s roar echoes through the Houses of Night, causing its denizens to scatter and hide. Set remains still, though his body is flooded with battle-fire. Years of nightly battle and practice prepared him for this moment, yet every conflict is new. The stakes are always high. Set's discipline keeps his senses keen, muscles ready for the decisive strike. ~~Apep~~ lunges, aiming for the child, prepared to swallow the source of all life. In a moment, Set pierces the mouth of ~~Apep~~ with his spear, pinning the serpent against the rock wall.

With a flash, Set's blade dismembers the serpent. The noise and discord return to stillness, and the barque continues its journey back to day.[61]

---

[61]. Kemetic depictions of the serpent typically represented him as in the process of dismemberment, so as to magically reinforce the defeat of the uncreator. Some modern-day reconstructionists honor this by depicting the serpent's name with a strikethrough.

Power is the most feared and sought-after quality in witchcraft. How many of us come to the study and practice of magic because we desired power? I loved stories of wizards, magicians, and witches with their capacity to summon and command great powers, to perform amazing feats, to befriend astounding beings, to enact their will through cunning.

Magic in practice has proven more subtle.

What is Power? The simplest definition for me begins with two capacities: to do and to influence. How disappointing a definition! So humble! Yet how profound is this simplicity. Power enables us to make change, to move, to manifest. These capacities are the cornerstones of sovereignty, autonomy, accountability, intimacy, responsibility, and authority.

Power is how we relate to the world. To enact my will, I need power. To create a joyful, happy home, I need power. To pay the bills, I need power. Without power, I am blown about by forces over which I have little influence.

At the same time, Power is vulnerable because it is not wholly dependent upon my thoughts and will. We influence and are influenced by each other. We have no way of opting out of that. When it comes to being alive, there is no "outside": if you're here, you're participating. You are one of many factors influencing a situation. We have some power, but not total and complete power. No one "chooses" to be oppressed, to be abused, to suffer chronic health problems. At the same time, we all have potential for agency, a choice in how to relate to circumstances.

I sat deeply with the complexity of this teaching when I worked as a case manager for people with criminal charges. My clients were highly diverse in terms of race, socioeconomic status, and types of crimes. What surprised me was the variety in how different clients responded to similar circumstances. For some, the idea of going to jail or becoming homeless was the worst thing imaginable. Others shrugged and accepted it with almost heartbreaking nonchalance. Still others were glad for it, preferring the structure of jail or the relative freedom of homelessness to the horrifying prospect of trying to live a "normal life." Those with a sense of agency had hope and a willingness to try. They were more active in finding help and seeking resources.

To keep this in context: these individual attitudes did not change the dearth of resources available. Those who wanted housing had to wait years before they got a chance at it, and some slept on the streets in the rain because that felt easier to bear than dealing with their post-traumatic stress disorder in a crowded shelter. Those who had supportive families and financial support were better connected to Power because they had more resources. Our current systems of incarceration are more likely to traumatize than heal long-standing mental illness. Former inmates emerge into an antagonistic society with few resources and no new skills.

Power is complicated when systems of authority, law, and economics coalesce as privilege and lift up the voices and influence of particular groups over others. This is what most think of as power, which Starhawk calls "power-over."[62] Power-over is the arrogation of others' power, the coercive imposition of will upon another. The ideal of a republic is to invest personal power to a representative who makes influential decisions for us, decisions that we could not implement on our own, yet all power is derived from the people. In practice, however, when systems or people accrue that kind of power, much effort becomes invested in maintaining the power, and it's easy to forget its origins.

Power-over constrains those who are "under" in their options to participate. Influence is contingent on subtle relational factors, mood, material resources, environment, and the historical moment. Our earliest lessons in navigating power-over relationships start with our caregivers. Being physically larger and our psychological source of security, identity, and safety, caregivers have significant influence over children, but children also shape their caregivers. Each child finds their strategies to gain attention, to manipulate, to push boundaries, to renegotiate, to resist, to surrender in the struggle to get needs met and become autonomous.

---

62. Starhawk, *Dreaming the Dark* (Boston: Beacon Press 1997).

Circling The Star

Problems arise when we are vested with Power due to social position, gender, race, or connections; weighted with responsibility that we cannot sustain and are unwilling to surrender because of the benefits that come with it. When I find myself clinging to titles, position, and outer credentials to bolster my authority, it is because my influence is already lessened. I've confused the external trappings with the internal state. When this happens, I risk slipping into power-over. As Ani DiFranco sings, "Every tool is a weapon / if you hold it right."[63]

All beings are worthy of respect, and we have every right to set expectations and not engage if they're not met. Recognizing each being's innate Power, no one has any obligation to meet our expectations. We cannot demand anything. We must gain others' willingness to cooperate.

Power and Earth

Earth, material existence, is the field upon which Power operates. Power also emerges from our relationship to the Earth that is our body and the land upon which we live.

Here are some images of Power:
- The wheel grips the road with friction, moving the car forward.
- The chick pecks open the shell from the inside, forcing its body out.
- The tree roots amidst the storm, bending and resisting the wind to keep itself intact.
- The wind pushes against the trees, spreading pollen and seeds.
- The crafter knits and purls yarn, shaping a sweater.
- The activist steps onstage, uninvited, to bring attention to her message, changing the speech the politician was about to make.
- The person considering suicide decides to ask for help.

My household teaches me much about Power. When I met my partner, I experienced him as more powerful because of his age, experience, and income. I deferred to him in decisions, even when he asked me explicitly to

---

63. Ani DiFranco, "My IQ," *Ani DiFranco New York March 30, 1995*.

give my own opinion. I projected upon him my ambivalence: wishing he would take control while resenting him for not anticipating and meeting all my needs. I treated him like he was a bad parent. I struggled to identify and ask for what I wanted, to take responsibility for how I showed up in the relationship. As I grow in personal Power, we have more equity and satisfaction in our relationship. We relate more as partners.

Other teachers have come into my life in the form of two rescue dogs. They're both trainable and stubborn. When I have food, I shape their behavior by rewarding them when they respond to my command with the desired action. They shape my behavior by figuring out what gets the desired response from me—one lays her toy on my lap so that I'll throw it. Outside the training zone, power becomes looser. Their willingness to follow commands ebbs when a cat is close.

One dog came with a lot of behavioral issues, including jumping on and gnawing on people. The more distressed he became, the more painful was his biting. When he jumped and chewed at me, I felt upset and frustrated and tried to regain control in ways that escalated his acting out. His distress fed on mine. One morning I realized: if I could keep myself calm, I would better elicit calm. For several weeks I made it my practice to calm myself when he acted out instead of responding to his behavior. Once I felt able to maintain this calm, I resumed my efforts to correct his acting out. This time, he was far more responsive.

This is the other side of Power, the one expressed by mountain, bone, and quiet winter. This quality of Power is one of negation, accessed through stillness, steadiness, silence, emptiness. This quality gathers strength, endures, waits with patience, focuses energy. It is the restraint of the warrior who saves energy for the precise strike that will collapse her opponent. It is the cleverness of the trickster who indicts foes with their own words.

Being and Doing are two ends of the polarity of Power. The mountain influences us with its presence. Planetary bodies exert gravitational influence due to the density of their mass. All of these forces interact, influence, and inform each other's behavior. When we do our personal and magical work

Circling the Star

in concert with other Beings, human or otherwise, the Power of the working grows.

Every point of the Iron Pentacle troubles us, which is what frees us. We do not run the Iron Pentacle and come out knowing the "right" ways to act. We will not always be gracious. We will cause harm, intended and not. The works in which we invest our heart and soul will receive criticism. Some of that criticism will come from petty in-fighting, jealousy, or cynicism, even when dressed up in beautiful language. Some of that criticism will be legitimate, things we need to hear to continue growing, even when expressed in blunt and rude language. The relationships and manifestations we create might seem worth the pain of all of this.

Walking in Power involves learning when to stop defending, when to acknowledge harm done, and when to stand for one's values. We can do all three at once. The fear that we'll lose Power when we admit mistakes or harm comes from the attachment to a well-polished surface image. Those who respond defensively to criticism, unwilling to accept responsibility but willing to blame others, foster polarization and antagonism. Adversaries create each other.

The following meditation helps connect with Power, drawing upon the image of Set that begins this chapter. Set is a Kemetic deity who has a long and complex history, connected with war, the desert, storms, outsiders, infertility, and chaos. In this chapter, Set is invoked in his aspect as the protector of Re, but he has also been the nemesis of his peers. In many ways he is Power, an amoral force that you'd rather have on your side. If you for any reason do not wish to work with Set, then you are welcome to simply focus on the images of Earth and not utilize the images related to Set or the Barque. If you do work with Set, you might leave him an offering of bread or beer.

Arrange your body into an engaged posture—stand if you are capable of standing for a long period of time; if not, sit upright with an engaged abdomen; if you cannot do that, engage whatever muscles you can in an alert posture. Slow your breathing down, and sink into the muscles that keep you in this posture. Notice too which muscles are not engaged. Sink into the bones that give your form structure and support.

Feel where your body meets the strength and solidity of Earth. Feel the connection of your feet or your body pressing down, and the Earth pressing back up. Breathe in the solid, deep, quiet, stable energy of Earth. Breathe into the Earth anything in you that needs support. Let the Earth help you hold your experience.

Imagine yourself astride the Barque of a Million Years, in darkness and silence, standing strong, waiting patiently for your work to present itself. Feel the discipline of stillness and openness, waiting, conserving energy. Feel the strength of your body that knows the work it needs to do. Invite into your body a sense of purpose. Let the energy of purpose fill your body and cause you to move. Be open to whatever movement your body wants to do, and know this movement is related to your work. Explore and play with the movement, making it bigger, faster, slowing it way down, making it smaller, until you have a sense of it. Return to stillness, and thank the earth for this teaching.

Journal, draw, or play with this movement. Watch yourself in the mirror doing the movement, or have a trusted ally watch you. There is information here, though it might not be immediately apparent.

POWER INFUSING PASSION: DISCIPLINE AND PLAY

The twins of Discipline and Play cultivate skill and expertise. Discipline is Power manifest as consistent action, self-restraint, and focus. To become a superlative piano player, I'm well served by submitting myself to daily practice and study. Whatever innate talent I have will not flourish spontaneously without this application of structure. Mood and bursts of energy and inspiration, or "arc fire," propel action, but unreliably.[64] To create something enduring, I need committed action. In European traditions of epic poetry, the poet begins by entreating the Muses to guide their words to tell the tale. The genius of the work is located outside of the Self. What is worth noting, however, is that this process of entreating is an active choice the poet makes. The poet shows up, asks inspiration, and then does their work.[65]

---

64. T. Thorn Coyle writes more of "arc fire" in *Evolutionary Witchcraft*.
65. Elizabeth Gilbert discusses this in greater depth in her TED Talk, "Your Elusive Creative Genius."

Circling The Star

My favorite image of discipline is the Eight of Pentacles from the Rider-Waite-Smith Tarot. The crafter appears intent upon their work. Stroke by stroke, the carving is made. In some versions of the card there is a lavish castle in the distance, evoking temptations of luxuries that distract from the demands of the work. The work itself looks quite boring. Many fail to manifest their grand visions, having spent all their efforts looking for shortcuts. A shadow teaching of this card is that this process of refinement and perfection becomes a fixation that impedes the process: discipline severed from Passion. Play reconnects the two.

Play is creative, purposeless activity. Play is about fun, but it has benefits. Through play, we can explore trying and failing at approaches to a problem, encouraging creative thinking and new mental pathways. Play releases stress and nourishes joyfulness. Studying and dutifully integrating a particular tradition or field of knowledge is a worthy pursuit, but when we begin to experiment and play with that body of knowledge, discover new applications or new shades of meaning, then we become experts and co-creators of that tradition. The Tarot image that connects to this is the Two of Pentacles, suggesting a juggler who keeps exchange moving—playful but with skill.

As a kid I used to make up dance routines to soundtracks, spend hours playing around with moving my body and dancing. I'd also spend hours writing. Either of these could have been Passions to which I dedicated myself, but ultimately I chose writing as my "thing." Not coincidentally, writing was the "thing" that my family and teachers encouraged. Growing up as a white male in Indiana in the 1980s, I probably picked up on the cultural antagonism toward male dancers. All the same, I continue dancing for fun, to de-stress and reconnect to my body and energy. I've "learned" skill in dancing by watching and imitating others and receiving some instruction, but in spite of my sweetest fantasies I'm unlikely to win a dance-off.

For me, dance stays in the realm of play, a quality I need and do not often allow myself. It's harder for me to allow play when doing my writing "thing," but it helps. That kind of play includes taking different approaches, silly or non-rational ones. Writing experiments like cut-ups, using tarot spreads, or fanfiction helps me get into a play mindset. Experimenting with language and plot sets aside the parts of myself that limit my creativity with their worries about how others will receive the work.

Studying witchcraft has taught me that Sticky One brings efficacy to magic. Sticky One engages in the tactile, fun elements of oils and incense, picking the right colors, singing songs, and waving tools in the air. Creating a sigil is fun, whether done through the play of chaos magic or the secret code systems of planetary squares. Magic also thrives with discipline: waking up at the right hour to do one's working, engaging in daily practice, applied study of the traditions and teachings.

Expertise is the resonance of grounded knowledge, of knowing from personal experience what works and what doesn't. The expertise of which I speak does not need to be announced or defended. No one can tear it down. If someone has something to offer that is contrary, it can only refine and add to your experience.

To differentiate within your passions, consider the following practices:
Think about the activities you like that feel like play, either current or in the past. Make some time for yourself to play this week.
Think about the Passions in which you want to develop skill or expertise. What is something you can do regularly to deepen your skill or move this forward?

SELF EMBODIED IN POWER: CHOICE

Power includes *our powers*, our myriad capacities "to do." We have as many potential powers as we have verbs. Power inhabits and moves through the body, the body's capacities and limitations to execute and do.

Western psychology and psychotherapy is increasingly exploring the benefits of somatic awareness and healing. So-called "talk" therapies have efficacy, but I find deeper transformations occur when we include the body. In a literal sense, all psychology is embodied. When I feel sad and think I'm a loser, my posture slumps over, I have feelings of pain or sadness in my body, my energy drops, I look at the ground and fail to sustain eye contact. One strategy to address this would be to interrogate the thoughts and restructure them to something more affirming. Another is to adjust my posture and take a deep breath. You might try that now, adjusting your posture and holding that while you read. What does that do to your mood and energy?

In sitting meditation, stillness of the body allows us to be with the deeper somatic experience. When I maintain a particular posture, attention to breath, and commitment to remain physically still regardless of what arises, I begin to see the play of thought, feeling, and sensation. I observe them without acting out my habitual behaviors. I sink beneath surface level awareness and reactivity into deeper spaciousness. I learn to tolerate uncomfortable and even painful sensations, which means that when I encounter them in life I am less avoidant.

Mindfulness meditation supports Power in that I can remain at choice in spite of provocations. Meeting distress and upset with stillness and self-observation increases discernment. Instead of losing my Power and reacting in ways that undermine myself, I consider new responses. This discernment, furthermore, helps me to step back from a hopeless situation and think about who set the terms.

In a negotiation, whoever sets the terms has already claimed the power. Parents know this when they create "forced choices" for their children: "You can clean your room now or after dinner." This empowers the child to have their own preferences and make a decision, while ultimately serving the parent's agenda. In both choices, the child cleans their room. This is appropriate for developing children who need limits for safety and limits to push against as they grow. When we become adults, however, our power is drained by unconscious submission to others' terms.[66]

In my early twenties, I was once walking to the train in downtown Chicago after work. A guy stopped me and offered to demonstrate his shoe cleaning supplies. Before I could answer, he spritzed the cleaning foam on my shoes and started scrubbing them, chatting with animation. After the first

---

65. In deference to people in the kink communities I used the phrase "unconscious submission." In BDSM, submission is an active choice, a voluntary exchange of power.

shoe, he let me know I owed him twenty dollars. "I'll let it go if you answer a riddle, though," he said.

I wondered aloud, "If I get the riddle wrong, will I owe you more money?" He changed the subject and kept cleaning. He was adept at creating forced choice situations—using false pretenses to elicit consent and then using that consent against me.

As he'd already started on the one shoe, I let him finish the second. It seemed I could either pay him and feel ripped off, or I could not pay him and risk a confrontation. Or I could play along with his riddle game and probably rack up more "costs." In the end, I decided to give him the twenty dollars. Though I knew I had been conned, I reclaimed my Power by consenting to participate in the terms that felt best to me. If I felt bolder, I might have refused altogether, but my shoes did look nice.

We encounter so many forced choices in relationships. A boss insists that you do something that goes against your personal judgment—the choice feels like either risking the job by refusing or risk endangering one's self by agreeing. A lover insists that they'll go back to drinking if you leave them for their abusive behavior—the choice feels like either being "responsible" for hurting the lover or agreeing to stay in a harmful relationship.

Forced choices exploit patterns of polarized thought and feeling, such as experiencing intense guilt if we do not set aside our own wishes and concede to those of loved ones. From the outside, the "black or white" quality of these choices seem irrational and harmful, but on the inside it is very difficult to hold that perspective. We get caught between charged parts of ourselves that narrow our conception of the world and what is possible within it. Moving toward one pole feels like a negation of the other, and it is hard to find a middle way. We feel caught.

"No way out" is a phrase that points to the Rusted facet of Powerlessness. In Powerlessness, we feel we are without ability or help. Our efforts seem to come to nothing, and we lack the energy to try. Powerlessness connects to feelings of despair, emptiness, numbness, anxiety, and rage. Psychologist Martin Seligman studied a phenomenon he called "learned helplessness" by separating groups of animals and subjecting them to shocks with various levels of control over how to stop the pain. Dogs who could stop the shock by pressing a lever later were able to adapt to a different situation and avoid being shocked. Dogs who could not stop the shock no matter what they did became passive and resigned, and when put in the later escapable shock scenario simply lay down to whimper.[67]

Powerlessness is a significant feature in mood disorders, anxiety, and trauma-related mental illnesses. It is also a barrier to creating health or wellness. People in Powerlessness suffer intense self-defeating thoughts, self-hatred, feelings of worthlessness. They become afraid to try anything, not wanting to have hope and then experience the pain of their hopes come to nothing. Without self-efficacy, we have no foundation for self-esteem.

Even more dangerous is becoming identified with Powerlessness. In this state, we believe we cannot be helped or change, though outwardly we may demand that which we think will fix all of our problems. We become fixated on cure-alls that do not really exist and reject any other kinds of help. We inadvertently sabotage efforts to help and blame the helper for the failure. "You should have called to remind me of our date, I can't keep track of things." Some balk and protest at any suggestion we can do things for ourselves, yet our outbursts of fear and anger are very effective at getting those around us to accommodate our needs. We wield significant influence, though on the surface most would agree that we are powerless.

We might have to work at it, but in every situation there is a kind of power, agency, and choice available to us. I'm definitely not saying the choices are pleasant, or we have control over everything that happens to us. We all have a range of abilities and some people need more support than others. Receiving help is itself a form of Power. Those actively working on recovery or receiving help develop ways to collaborate with their care providers. They could actively voice their needs and limitations, make requests, plan to accommodate for known issues.

---

[67]. Martin Seligman and Steven Maier, "Failure to Escape Traumatic Shock," *Journal of Experimental Psychology*, Volume 74, Issue 1, 1967 (Washington, DC: American Psychological Association).

When anchored in stillness and Power, we can look at forced choice, polarization, and helplessness from a larger perspective. The following is an exercise that I do with some clients who are struggling with an internally polarized issue:

Plant your feet on the ground and adjust your posture. Find a posture that feels firm but not too rigid. Close your eyes and call to mind an inner conflict that feels stuck and difficult to resolve, particularly one in which it feels like two parts of you are at war. Think about how you can separate this conflict into two parts. You might come up with different names or phrases to encapsulate the polarization, or notice what feelings are predominant on one side versus the other.

Choose one of these parts to work with first. Let the other part know that you will give it attention, but for the moment you need it to stand aside. Focus on the first part and call its energy into you. Breathe it into your body. Notice the felt sense of it. Notice what emotions or thoughts arise. Notice if it has color, texture, sound, or brings up other images.

Stretch out one of your hands as though you are holding something. You will keep it in this position for some time, so you might rest the arm on your leg. Gather the energy of this part from your being into your hand. Imagine a symbol that represents the energy and make sure all of it is out of your body and in the symbol on your hand. If you are stuck on a symbol, imagine it as a sphere of energy.

Now turn toward the other part of the struggle. Breathe that into your body. Be with the felt sense of it. Notice what arises. Try to spend as much time with this as you did with the part before. Then hold out your other hand, and send all the energy from this part into that hand.

Now sit holding these parts in each hand. Experiment with holding them out. Notice the weight of each, the temperature, the texture, or any relationship between the two parts. If you notice at this point that you are having other feelings or trying to analyze the process, ask those thoughts and feelings to step aside for a moment. Connect to the open, compassionate power of your heart. Ask your heart for guidance on the way forward.

Now bring your hands together, letting these parts touch. Bring your hands to your heart and let these energies return to you. Whether an answer has emerged or not, thank yourself and your parts for showing up to this process.

Power Connecting to Sex: Generosity, Gratitude, Mystery

Power is the last point on the clockwise circle of Iron. Having harnessed pure life force into the expression of Self, deepened into passionate connection with the world, affirmed its autonomy and worthiness, and become energy to manifest, it now cycles back to pure life force to close the circumference. The energy has fundamentally changed. Each time we run the Pentacle, we inscribe it anew.

In this way, this movement connects to dying and releasing form. It is the moment when Power expresses in service to a principle beyond personhood. Here we release attachment to outcome. As was written in the Thelemic *Book of the Law*: "For pure will, unassuaged of purpose, delivered from the lust of result, is every way perfect."[68] In this movement, Power extends itself beyond the personal in generosity, gratitude, and mystery.

Generosity is the extension of one's efforts and resources for the benefit of others. Receiving influence is a form of validation and connection. To accept your influence is to recognize your worthiness. Even if we disagree, we can listen and consider the other person's view before stating why we do not think it's useful. What disempowers is when we reject, outright ignore a person, repeatedly dismiss their view, mock or insult the person, and so forth.

Looking at what we hoard is useful in cultivating generosity. For example, I spent years shyly listening and holding my opinion on things, rarely volunteering my time and talents to help. Consciously, I believed I had little worth saying and nothing worth offering. Eventually I came to see this as being stingy with my life force. I allowed others to carry the conversations and make all the effort. At my worst I was critical of them for not doing it "right." Standing on the outside and disparaging people's efforts felt safer than being the one to step into the center and try. Becoming more generous meant speaking more, offering more, volunteering more, and taking more

---

68. Aleister Crowley, *Liber AL vel Legis*, http://www.sacred-texts.com/oto/engccxx.htm..

action. The more I understand the challenges of leadership, the more generosity I feel toward the perceived failures of others.

Others have opposite tendencies: to insistently take control of projects and processes, dominate conversations, and shut down criticism. For these folks, generosity may look like giving space for others to speak and step up, to acknowledge and validate other ideas, to encourage others to take over and do the work their way.

It is said that we grow what we lack when we give it away. There is truth here, but giving away must be voluntary and open-hearted, not coerced or guilted out of us. When others begin to take our generosity for granted, resentment is inevitable. No one is entitled to your energy or labor. Practicing generosity is much easier when we are otherwise being fairly compensated for our labor. Contracts determined between parties in equal dignity are life-affirming and should be open to negotiation when they're not.[69]

We rarely fully know the extent of our influence. We do the best with what we have and know, and with luck we may get glimpses of the impact of our actions. Think about someone who's touched your life deeply. Think about all the people who have taught you something. Think about the passing comments, the writings, the speeches, the beautiful music, the art, the acts of kindness and generosity, the acts of cruelty, all that has woken you up. Do these people know how much they've impacted you? What if you've been as impactful in your own way? What if there are hundreds of people out there who have or will be touched by your influence in ways you will never know?

Think, too, of all the efforts that brought this moment to you. Think of all the labor that has gone into shaping your environment. Think of the generations of ancestors whose lives made yours possible, in ways known and unknowable. Think of the dead whose genetic material is given life through you, though in a different form. All of this leads me to gratitude. When I

---

[69], I distinguish between the personal dimension of generosity and social interventions to redistribute wealth equitably. Participating in a nation-state is a somewhat consensual contract, in that many of us do not "choose" citizenship. If you benefit from the wealth, resources, and public goods of your country, then paying income toward their maintenance is part of the contract.

consider the overwhelming breadth of this web of influence, I feel thankful for all these Beings who have shaped my life.

You are a part of a great process that is unfolding, the being whose totality is called by some God Hirself. You are a thought in God Hirself's mind, seeking to be known, refined, and expressed. You are a feeling flowing through God Hirself's heart, seeking to be felt, recognized, and connected. You are a cell in God Hirself's body, part of an enormous and mysterious organ. You do not have to trust that God Hirself has "a plan" for you, for you are co-architect of the plan.

Within your life is the Work you came here to do. You may follow the thread of Work deeply today and discover in a year that it all seems like bullshit, but it's bull shit that fertilized the soil of your becoming. Waiting to know The Answer before you act is almost a guarantee that you will never learn The Answer. Learn by doing. Do, and see what happens.

The following exercises offer some strategies for Doing:

- ❖**Generosity:** *For a week, pay attention to where you expend energy and where you conserve it. Observe how you behave in social situations, at work meetings, in classes, in community. See if you can identify any themes of action or restriction in your behavior. Then the next week, practice changing one behavior with an intention of generosity. Some ideas: Make eye contact with strangers and say hello. Pause to connect with someone, even when you're in a hurry. Compliment someone's efforts. Acknowledge someone's opinion. In a conversation, offer one perspective and then listen to three or four others before offering another. Notice who is left out of social spaces and extend an invitation.*

- ❖**Gratitude:** *Take time to contemplate all the people and beings who have contributed to your life. At meals, reflect on all the labor, plants, or animals whose life force contributed to the meal you're about to eat. Thank someone who helped you, or who plays a meaningful role in your life. Think of one person who has given you much and write a letter thanking them for all they've done for you, or to you, that has helped you become who you are.*

❖***Mystery:*** *Find some time when you can be quiet and settle in. Slow down your breathing, and ask your Sticky One to help you experience all the connections and influences you have felt in your life, to sense your being in the totality called God Hirself. Spend some time with this, and then align with your God Soul. Feel the connection between Sticky One and God Soul, and ask to be shown something of your impact in the world. Notice any judgments that come up around your impact, but for the moment simply see if you can feel that energy rippling away from you, influencing others. If you wish, pray to be helped in making your influence one more congruent with the world you want to manifest.*

POWER HELD IN PRIDE: SURRENDER

Taking action is vulnerable and uncertain. The likelihood is we'll experience criticism or opposition. If we're unwilling to accept this possibility, that will interfere. These unwilling parts often believe themselves incapable of tolerating the pain of experiencing it. While it's possible to push onward in spite of this resistance, those parts of us need acknowledgment and care. We must accept our fragilities with our strengths. The effort to be strong every day takes a toll on the soul. We need rest days. Weightlifting weakens muscle by tearing it apart. What makes muscle stronger is the post-exercise recovery period. We need safe spaces to be vulnerable, vent, cry, feel weak.[70]

When we push onward and neglect those vulnerable feelings, we move into the Gilded quality called Force. Force is an aggressive, hostile enactment of effort in the world. Force walks over boundaries, yells, screams, turns red in the face. Force resists compromise or listening. Force encounters a giant boulder on the path and starts shoving, heedless of the pain, until either the boulder moves or it's pushed itself into exhaustion and injury. Force is a narrow gaze, unable to recognize or admit that simply climbing over the boulder is a viable option. To Force, the mere presence of the

---

70. "Safe space" has become, ironically, a weaponized term. The world is not a safe space, nor do I think our public institutions should be. We do need relationships and spaces where we can feel safe to support better participation in the unsafe world.

boulder is offensive and anything other than the course of action it's decided would be a failure, an admission of weakness.

Force has subtle expressions as well. Those on the receiving end of Force experience helplessness, vulnerability, hurt, invalidation, and indignation as the person in Force plows their agenda forward. Force detaches personal will from the field of relationship, sometimes from any sense of groundedness. Often, people in Force don't realize that their behavior is so hurtful or destructive. Internally they too feel powerless, impatient, vulnerable, hurt, and invalidated and believe that their responses are justified. Force says, "I need this to work!" "Why is this taking so long?" "Why's everything such a problem?"

An antidote to Force is Surrender. As a Quaker-Pagan friend of mine once asked, however, "Surrender to what?" Often witches and Pagans see surrender as steeped in Christianity and not conducive to a Pagan cosmology. What I seek is not giving up my power, will, and agency so much as releasing my attachment to how things should be.

Let's return to the image of a boulder blocking my path. The boulder's presence is not a personal affront. The boulder simply exists. Most of the time, the boulder has no effect on me. Only now, when I have this desire to get to the other side and it happens to be on the path I wanted to take, do I have feelings about it. I experience outrage, despair, and blame. That is what I want to surrender.

What does the energy of "Surrender" feel like for you? You might let the word sink into your core and fill your energy bodies. What in you opposes this quality? What are the reasons for this? If "Surrender" is unworkable, you might try the words "Sink" (as in "descend"), "Accept," or "Release" instead. If none of these work, perhaps the effort will help you find something that does.

The tricky part is deciding "to what" you will surrender. Here are some ideas:

❖**Surrender to What Is:** Look at the obstacles and limitations against which you're pushing. Look at the effort you're expending and how much progress that effort gets you. Look at the climate, your mood, the social temperature. Look at the larger economic, cultural, and social contexts. Let limitations be limitations. Stop pushing the immovable boulder and accept its presence. Accept the anger and anxiety that seem ever-present. Accept that your coworker talks over you in spite of how many times you've asked them to stop. Accept that technology is changing your industry. Don't let go of your goals, values, and desires, but for a moment recognize the limits on what you can control. These things exist, they are part of "what is," and will not change for you. What becomes possible when you stop spending energy pushing against these seemingly fixed realities?

- **Surrender to God Soul:** When you feel stuck and lost, you can breathe your distress up to God Soul with a request for guidance. Listen for an answer, or simply move forward with the possibility that God Soul will guide you through your instinct. If your desire brings you into suffering repeatedly, surrender it entirely to God Soul. Ask for help discerning what of this desire is truly your Work and what needs to be released.

- **Surrender to Deity:** In the past I've tried to surrender my life and will to deity, and most gods seemed uninterested in that. Polytheist friends caution that this is a rash and dangerous promise to make. I find that the gods respond best to me when I explain, "This is what I'm trying to do and these are the limitations I'm encountering." Try dedicating the problem and its outcome to a deity. Listen for guidance, or take whatever action seems appropriate. Attend to whatever happens in response to your actions as though it were a message from your god(s). This is more about being in dialogue with the gods than receiving a moralistic judgment.

- **Surrender to Practice:** In my work with Morningstar Mystery School, we are constantly practicing. Everything is a practice. Practice brings us to presence. Practice opens us to magic and the possibilities that escape our current ego awareness.

When you feel stuck and overwhelmed, pick a practice and bring it to the situation. The Iron Pentacle is useful for this. What happens when you run Sex energy while dealing with the problem? How does your sense of Pride affect the problem? What facets of Self are "hooked" into the problem? What

Power do you have in this situation? Working with the elements, you might practice observing thoughts, feelings, bodily states, and energy fluctuations in relationship to the problem.

Each facet has something to offer, so try not to worry about which choice is "right." Pick a practice and commit to it for a period of time. Depth and sincerity of practice is more useful than throwing several approaches at the problem and giving up when encountering resistance.

To Jung is attributed the statement, "the experience of the Self is always a defeat for the ego."[71] The ego releases its strategies in the face of the Self's profound wisdom. In this context, Surrender is not resignation, not simply giving up and falling into despair. It is an act of will, a willingness to experience something new and unplanned. When in Force, Surrender feels like an abdication, but it truly brings us back to Power. Instead of destroying myself against the boulder, I suddenly glimpse an opening that lets me step around and through. Or I give up on this path, turn around, and have an adventure finding a better route.[72]

Reflect on a problem that you've been stuck with for some time. Take a piece of paper to fold in thirds lengthwise. On the left side, write down all the strategies you've tried to solve the problem. In the middle, write down how effective this strategy was. On the right side, write down the unwanted, painful, or frustrating consequences of the strategy.

What about the problem seems immovable? What remains stuck no matter what you do? Take another piece of paper and free-write about this, or draw a picture that symbolizes the immovable aspects of the problem.

Look at the forms of Surrender discussed above. Does one form of Surrender appeal to you in this situation? Commit to practicing this form of Surrender when you encounter one of these immovable facets of the problem for the next week to month, depending on how frequently you encounter the problem. Keep track of the results.

---

71. C. G. Jung, *Collected Works of C.G. Jung*, Volume 14 (New Jersey: Princeton University Press, 1970).
72. Unfortunately, once the ego sees that this strategy works, it may try to co-opt the Surrender as another tool to get what it wants. Surrender is about releasing egoic attachment, and won't be faked. If we can't consciously make it happen, sometimes the best we can do is accept that a part of us is unable to surrender at this time.

Power, Exalted in Liberty

Hail Knhum-Re,
Ram-headed, Sun-crowned.
Your hands render beauty
From stone, enspirit
Matter, drum our hearts.
Infusing ankh with touch,
You liberate us in joy.
Because of You our will
Shapes the matter of life.

With hands in clay and head crowned by solar fire, Knhum-Re earths the creative source, imbuing his work with its own essential freedom. Without the ankh of Re, we would be golems of clay walking the earth without personal will. Our solar birthright charges us with Liberty.

The symbol of Saturn is the cross of matter above the sickle of soul, suggesting the feeling of constriction and oppression of the soul within the confines of materiality. The circle of Spirit is absent from this symbol, but as Ivo Dominguez Jr. points out in his book *Practical Astrology for Witches and*

Pagans, this could symbolize either a deficit or excess of that energy. We are pure limitless light and energy, but we need this experience of material existence, hardness, limitation. Though at times this feels like a prison, it is what affords us the capacity for differentiation, self-awareness, and will.

Thus the pain of separation and limitation need not be a sign of a degraded world, rather a necessary condition for our becoming. As Knhum-Re fashions us into enspirited beings of clay, Saturn sunders us from the wholeness of God Hirself that we may find Liberty and offer our own wholeness back to Hir. We have the potential to mature and claim power in our lives. This liberation, rooted in Power and Earth, comes from discipline, training, endurance, and responsibility. These qualities often have a poor reputation as themselves burdensome restrictions of the soul, oppressing the "free" spirit. When chosen consciously and cultivated, however, they fortify the freedom of Spirit. Our Spirit can more fully express itself through our expanded powers, our inner authority, and our capacity to do.

Liberty is the exaltation of the body and the grounding of Spirit. It is the apotheosis of the journey of the witch through the pentacles of Iron and Pearl. Liberty is complete differentiation with connection, the Peacock—fully emerged and turned toward God Hirself in love and honor. All children, all acts of art aspire to this state of autonomous being, separate yet whole.

What terrifies is the lack of certainty. In a state of Liberty, we may listen to feedback and guidance from a variety of sources but ultimately the choice and responsibility of action remains centered within. Hence the need for the fullness of the Pearl Pentacle. Knowledge and Wisdom support us in making the best decisions we can perceive in the moment. Love and Law keep us connected and acting in good faith. From this, we can act upon our will and express the deepest yearnings, the fullest desires, the most profound speakings of our vision into the world. Our very footsteps shape the earth, as the earth shapes us. Nothing is guaranteed but neither are we bound by expectations. There is no central authority to judge our actions.

In Liberty, we are the fullest expression of the longing of the earth. The soil itself desires to be known and loved, to experience breath and starlight. The grasses and trees long to write poetry. The skies seek to paint and be admired for their beauty. Whether other forms of being are capable of any of these feats, as humans we certainly are, and as the children of earth and sky we contain a unique seed of longing that wants fruition.

Liberty is a state of interdependence, for we are social animals who have needs that require others: needs around belonging, intimacy, social recognition, status, and growth. As a child, I needed the love and structure of my caregivers and teachers to survive. As an adult, I crave sex, intimacy, respect, and friendship, and yet I want these exchanged fully and consensually. We all have different levels of ability to meet our needs, and our parts of self are often in different stages of maturation.

In this state we are fully realized, autonomous beings who are complete and whole unto ourselves. We know our power and feel our feet on the ground. We choose with whom to associate and what strictures to follow, knowing that we are beholden to none and none are obligated to us. No being has authority over us that we do not yield; neither do we have power over others that is not yielded to us.

To an extent, we all need others to survive. A network of Liberty with interdependence is more desirable than the atomizing individualism that afflicts us today. We run into problems when people have more Liberty than they do Power. This is one of the failings of capitalism today. The lack of equal access and equal social power means we do not equally benefit from freedom.

As an example: during the 1980s, a wave of reforms led by the Reagan administration in the United States shut down several long-term mental healthcare wards and sent patients in need to outpatient community health centers that could not provide the same level of care and support. This increased the liberty of the formerly institutionalized patients without a commensurate increase in material and social support. Many chronically mentally ill individuals end up living on the streets.

Liberty is freedom from external restraint, requiring internal restraint as a counterbalance. In his essay, "Freedom is a Two-Edged Sword," Jack Parsons defined the two edges of the sword of freedom as "liberty and responsibility," and added: "Both edges are exceedingly sharp and the weapon is not suited to casual, cowardly or treacherous hands."[73] These two edges mean that we do whatever we wish so long as we take responsibility for the outcome. A lot of folks seem to want Liberty without this responsibility. They say hurtful, thoughtless, or offensive things and then claim their freedom of speech is under attack when criticized in turn. They want to consume without worrying about the consequences for the planet.

Liberty without responsibility is a toxic form of self-expression, one that hurts people and relationships and narrows life. When we expect to receive without giving, we are in for a surprise when it turns out those in our relationships stop giving. Western Esoteric magic has a history of commanding the obedience of deity and spirit to enact the magicians' will, but even dominance is a form of relationship that our spirit contacts could sabotage if we lack respect.

Liberty is terrifying in this way. The witch and magician do not rely upon messianic figures or scapegoats for salvation. Fortune and ill favor fall alike on our shoulders with none to spare us, at least not without cost.

One facet of the quest for Liberty is to free one's self of the constant demand to hustle for physical and material needs. Much of the energy and will spent on this plane is toward this end, either through the immanent path of acquisition or through the transcendent path of renunciation. The Body of Shu shows the courses of these paths through the tarot suit of Coins. As always, parsing this in dualism illustrates pathways of energy movement in the journey.

---

73. Jack Parsons, "Freedom is a Two-Edged Sword," http://www.bibliotecapleyades.net/bb/babalon210.htm.

The Tarot Suit of Coins & The Journey of Liberty

Ace of Coins

All potentiality and need meets here in the nexus. The Ace of Coins represents the capacity for all needs to be satisfied without effort, all efforts to be already received. Birth and death, shelter and Liberty, all coexist at once. No effort is required, nothing is needed, so long as one is content to remain.

Two of Coins

An experience of lack spurs the Hustler into relationship with others to gain through trade. The Hustler recognizes they have something unique to offer to acquire the resources and materials they desire, in an ongoing exchange in which giving and receiving are simultaneous.

The Hustler returns to the eternal cycle of exchange, renouncing profit and embracing equal exchange, discovering the mysteries of generosity, in which by giving one receives.

Three of Coins

Having discovered the possibility of profit through trade, the Hustler discovers that working in tandem with a group increases their output and their profit significantly. They may become a supervisor, profiting from the collective labor of others, or one of the laborers coming to resent the supervisor.

The Hustler engages in labor as a form of community engagement and connection, realizing that by serving their needs are met, and by working they honor the spirit interred in matter.

FOUR OF COINS

Having discovered the pleasures of profit and acquisition and the possibility of exploitation, the Hustler begins to keep careful track of their resources and stringently budget to make sure their needs are met.

The Hustler begins to offer their wealth to all who need, letting go of rigidity and liberating their assets to the rhythms of the world. They may engage in restrictive practices of self-denial to increase mastery over instinctive urges.

FIVE OF COINS

The Hustler diverges and meets. Either they further suffer from deprivation, oppression, and class exploitation and must turn toward others' generosity for bare survival, or, they benefit from class privilege, social capital, and luck, and give to another to expiate their guilt.

Stepping out of systems of profit and dominance, the Hustler turns toward spiritual service, tending the needs of themselves and others to support them in moving closer to the Spirit within matter. Experiences of deprivation enhance the spiritual quest.

SIX OF COINS

The unfairness perpetuates as the Hustler becomes more successful and realizes, now that their needs are met, that they are in a position to determine who benefits more from the collective profit. On the other facet of the path, the Hustler experiences unfair distribution of resources and further realizes that those with power and wealth may distribute resources based on whim.

Continuing to explore the conditions of capital and exchange, the Hustler observes the intrinsic partiality and unfairness of systems of trade, exchange, and wealth. The Hustler questions why some must lose while others gain, and what their place is in this system. They imagine the possibility of being outside or bringing balance to the system.

SEVEN OF COINS

Having confronted success or poverty, the Hustler takes stock in what was gained or lost to date and must decide whether to continue the path or move elsewhere. What work will satisfy their needs and free them for other pursuits?

Remembering that the world is abundant and offers all that is needed, the Hustler begins to question the necessity of work and labor.

EIGHT OF COINS

The Hustler dedicates themself to the cultivation and mastery of a trade. Labor itself becomes rewarding, more important than the immediacy of reward.

The Hustler returns to discipline and labor as an end in itself, a way of enspiriting the material world rather than acquiring material wealth. Discipline informs greater distance from the restless needs of the body, allowing more energy to move toward spiritual pursuit.

NINE OF COINS

Having mastered the material realm, the Hustler has complete self-esteem. They know they can receive whatever they need, whenever they need. They have all the access and resources they need to survive.

The Hustler releases first their commitment to place and property, entrusting themselves to the vicissitudes of the world. Early successes help them to know they can have their needs met without the trappings of wealth.

TEN OF COINS

The Hustler has mastered the material realm and is awash in resources. They create a zone of safety and privilege for their families, children, and loved ones. They risk experiencing this as a cloistered, defensive wall, closed off from generosity and fixated on protection and increasing wealth for wealth's sake. The Hustler may have mastered the exterior world but still feel enslaved to pleasure, need, and materiality.

Circling The Star

Every journey through the Iron and Pearl Pentacles shakes new material loose, frees up bound energy, widens the cracks in long-calcified patterns. We become more conscious, and thus more capable of Liberty. It is a trick on the ego. All this allure of power and freedom, and instead we wake up to our own stuckness, our own pettiness, our own limitations. We begin to see how much we give away power and freedom. We begin to see how much even our fantasies pull us away from what is possible in this moment.

Our awareness of the bindings on our power and freedom expands the more we accrue. The less I blamed others for my personal dissatisfactions, the more I noticed the way I kept parts of myself locked up, isolated, cast away, suppressed. I noticed how often I wanted to put others down for being what I feared and desired. I noticed how often I restricted rather than expanded, and as I began to see what violence that did to myself, it became less tolerable to watch it enacted upon others. Divesting myself of internal limitations helps me to see more clearly the external bindings.

Such freedom is profoundly vulnerable. Asserting myself in a new way, I may be beset by praise and criticism and it's unclear which is valid, to what and whom I should attend. I see how often people go unrecognized or hated in life who end up canonized after death, and indeed the meaning of history shifts with time. There are no unqualified heroes, sinless saints, valueless villains.

The more we claim our Power and resonate Liberty, the more shackles of any sort become offensive extensions of our own burdens. When I liberate a part of me that has been long burdened by fear or shame, its monstrousness meets the hand of Love and transforms. Oppressing and imprisoning others is not a route to freedom. The slow decline of the United States's empire was woven into its origins of genocide and slavery. It grew with astonishing speed and wealth because it had so much "free" land and labor, such that once those resources stopped being free, it could not stop. It turned to whatever cheap labor was available, and moved outward to claim access to cheap resources. The wealth of a few arose on the backs of thousands, and the privileged and powerful were taught to resent the people who were crushed underfoot, and passed this to their children.

Survival is not enough. Our material wants and needs matter, but we are more than that as well. Celebrating a life of joy and ease while others bleed and die for our luxuries is a toxin to the soul, it is another layer of the harm we do to ourselves and the planet. We treat our precious land, water, and air as dumping grounds for waste and take what we need. We narrow our gaze to the smallest unit, the individual person, the particular race, and prioritize those needs over the entire sphere of the planet. We pull ourselves out of relationship with the wider fabric, we disrupt the order of Ma'at, all for the appearance of Liberty that material wealth and technology allows us. As people and cultures we have sundered the material from its spiritual roots, racking up debt, and the collectors are coming to take what we owe.

This is a great sorrow, for those of us who must pay the debt are not the ones who first began to accrue it. Generations before us set upon the path that has led to civil unrest and global climate change, and it may be too late to stop or undo the damage. We cannot wait. We must move toward liberation right now. We must turn toward the groaning of the earth and the tears of the oppressed among us. We must find a chain to break, and break it. We must find what is imprisoned and help it to become free. Our wildness calls for us to remember it and cease trying to train, entrap, and cage it for the purposes of simple profit and comfort. Within our soul, our deepest values call for our work.

It is appropriate for me to take care of what I can, as much as I can, so I can better be of service. After ten years of dedicated spiritual practice and self-work I realize my voice has become stronger, clearer, and more calm. I'm less defensive when called out on mistakes or offenses, more educated about problems, and better able to speak out.

Trying to change and control my thoughts and feelings was an avoidance of conflict. Instead of confronting what in the world was harming me and my loved ones, I tried to change myself to make it okay. And in turn, my avoidance of confronting and working for change in the external world was a strategy for avoiding inner discomfort and distress. If I thought I was in control of myself, then I would not have to deal with feelings of failure, overwhelm, defeat, or being out of control. The "control" I had was contingent on keeping my life somewhat small, adapting constantly to others' impositions, and focusing on issues that were not important to me.

Control is an illusion. When I cannot accept my inner experience, I attempt to control everything around me to keep things calm. When I cannot accept my outer experience, I attempt to control my thoughts and feelings through painful and constricting strategies of self-denial and suppression. The desire for control arises from our deep need to feel safe. Sticky One needs to know it will be cared for, it won't be abandoned, and yet this need comes from the knowing that eventually we will die, everything changes, and everything will be lost.

My sense is that Sticky One needs our conscious presence and connection to Earth's endurance. Our real physical needs matter, as they support presence. What Sticky One wants is for us to be present with its experience, attending and not abandoning it to terror, violence, starvation, and loneliness. When we are children, we need other people to bring loving witness so our Sticky One will experience safe, secure attachment. We still need this loving witness to help us internalize it for ourselves.

The body is a wild thing, a beautifully formed animal that houses the totality of my being. The body is free and frees us. When our minds want to create suffering and limitation, want to narrow possibilities or terrify, our bodies offer an altar of witnessing. When I am present within my body, all my fears and desires are simply sensations playing out within me. Some are only in my mind, and I can tell because my body does not respond to them.

In witchcraft, the path of liberation differs from what is often associated with Eastern approaches. We do not necessarily seek to leave the cycle of death and rebirth, or to disconnect from material existence and merge into a wholly spiritual plane of being. Khnum-Re offers the work of braiding the material and the spiritual, forming reality in the images of our creation. According to Gordon White in *Star.Ships*, the ritual techniques to facilitate spiritual immortality among the stars has a profoundly long and deep relationship to humanity, perhaps an inheritance from our oldest ancestors.[74]

74. Gordon White, *Star.Ships: A Prehistory of the Spirits* (London: Scarlet Imprint, 2016).

Some say that the Earth creates witches to enact the balance it needs, like antibodies responding to bacterial infection. What I notice among so many witches today is a focus on the power and freedom of the body. We need our wildness back and our precious materiality, but with full consciousness. We need our God Souls in deep relationship with the body. Wildness and ferality are not easy for me, whose personality has always tended toward the cerebral, yet coming into my body continues to set me free. All the fear and anxiety of not-knowing disappear. My body instinctively learns the terrain and when aligned with God Soul is a profound teacher.

In Liberty, the energies of Iron and Pearl resonate within the body. We learn the points through living them, sensing them, playing with them. Too much faith in mental certainty gets in the way of this mystery. Set aside my words. Feel the star in your body, the points at each extremity. Let the hot energy of Iron pour through you. Let the cool energy of Pearl beautify and refine you. You are formed in beauty, held in the hand of Love.

With your freedom, what would you make of this world?

THE BEGINNING IS THE END IS THE BEGINNING

Few better symbols represent witchcraft better than the Pentacle, with its first-glance simplicity that increases in complexity until once again resolving into a profound clarity. A nonlinear symbol; there is no beginning and no end. We enter, move through the energy, and step out if needed. Every apocalypse is also a creation story: eternal, unfolding process.

Cosmology informs psychology. The stories we tell about the nature of existence and the creation of the gods or humans are stories we tell about the nature of consciousness. What we believe about the nature of the cosmos dictates the kinds of questions we ask of ourselves and the dreams we dream.

Esoteric psychology is useful for the prescriptive nature of spiritual work. Yet if our beliefs about the psyche do not cohere with descriptive scientific research or simple human observation, then it's time to ask some serious questions about the nature of our practice. Thus throughout this book I have included perspectives from Western psychology to complement, rather than compete with, the views discussed.

While writing this book, I have contemplating the question of "Why do we run the Pentacles?" I have been instructed in the model of the Triple

Soul, the Elements, and reverence for the gods, ancestors, and other spirits. Much of my practice over the past ten years has been cleansing and becoming more and more aligned with my God Soul.

My belief is that I have been transforming my body and my life into a worthy residence of God Soul, the most divine part of me. The Pentacles play a role in that, but I also believe they play a role in answering the question "What next?" As the animal, human, and divine souls work in greater concert, the imagined hierarchy between divine impulse and base instinct begins to dissolve.

The transformation of the Iron Pentacle works these edges. The qualities that arouse such fear and longing in us, which often fall into our most abusive relations with each other, become the birthright of our divine selves. No longer at war with my desire for Sex, Pride, Self, Power, and Passion, I make them sacred. Because of this sacred self-honesty, the qualities of Love, Law, Knowledge, Wisdom, and Liberty resonate from me.

The work is what makes it so. All the raw materials are here already. When you purposely take up the tool and begin the work, you wake up. When you put down the tool and forget about it, you drift back to sleep. This is true whether it's your first day of spiritual practice or your second decade.

This sense of time and spiritual practice occasionally throws me into a moment of despair and disillusionment. I began studying witchcraft because I wanted to fix myself and end my suffering. Eventually I came to see that believing I needed to be fixed was a cause of my suffering. There is work to do, but doing so now seems to be about aligning myself with the deeper currents and patterns of the world. My personal struggles are microcosms of global ones, and they may be more entwined than is comfortable to admit.

As I write this, it is clear to me that we are in a time when our patterns of avoidance are contributing to our harm. We are approaching a true crisis, one that could plunge us more deeply into destruction, or one that could be the forest fire that clears the way for rejuvenation. We need as many people as possible to be awake and doing their work. I hope this book is of help to yours.

Terms Used In This Book, And How

I believe many arguments could be avoidable if those involved took the time to define their terms. Whether you agree with my specific definitions, my hope is that the following will provide context so that you better understand my perspective.

Awareness: The faculty by which beings apprehend their nature and interact with their environment. Some theorists propose that consciousness is a quality inherent to all matter, and certain organizations of matter accrue greater capacities for consciousness based on complexity. (Synonyms: being, presence, consciousness.)

Body: Enspirited, ensouled matter capable of awareness. Subject to natural, material law and the passage of time. Expresses life-affirming instincts that may be overridden, misinterpreted, or ignored by the mind. Closely related to the instinctive animal soul. Site of sensory information and the material aspects of Self, including the organic brain and hormones.

Divine Twins: Twin deities of divine opposition and dialectic relationship, the first born from God Hirself. When they meet in their tension of opposites, the synthesizing third form arises, known as the Peacock. They express both the experience and the illusion of dualism.

Ego: Mental structure that provides experience of identity and continuity that supports action in the world and actualization of capacities. Executive function of the personality.

God Hirself: Victor and Cora Anderson passed down the story that God Herself is the Star Goddess, the source and fabric of all being, from whom the cosmos emerged and unto whom they will return. To further highlight the genderqueer nature of this deity, the gender-neutral pronoun "Hir" is employed.

God Soul: The part of the soul that is closest to God Hirself. The oldest part of the soul, containing memories and wisdom from lifetimes. Our personal divinity. It is generally perceived as a sphere floating above the head, though with practice and diligent efffort it may descend briefly or permanently to surround and interpenetrate the skull. Also known as Sacred Dove or Sacred Falcon.

Life-force: The creative and enlivening energy of a living being. Analogous to concepts from other spiritual and cultural systems such as ankh, prana, mana, awen, or qi. In the Iron Pentacle, life-force is also Sex energy.

Matter: Solid, dense energy that is relatively stable in form and subject to the laws of physics. That which is external to, and apprehended by, the senses. Of Latinate origin, *mater* connects back to mother; mothers make us matter, and matter is mother to awareness.

Mind: Organizing principle of awareness that draws upon experience and observation to create cognitions, stories, rules, language, and logical inferences. Inclusive of the ego and the rational soul. Able to generate original conceptualizations and possibilities for being in the world; also prone to reductivity, dualism, and fixation on ideas of the world that do not cohere with lived experience.

Self: The entirety of an individual existence and experience, both conscious and unconscious, known and unknown, personal and transpersonal. A loosely-bounded physical and psychic organism in which there are many parts and subsystems.

Shining Body: The part of the soul that is most rational, and thus said to be the most human. It surrounds the body in a larger egg shape, extending several inches out. This part is social, giving and receiving information. Also known as Talker.

Spirit: Animating, enlivening, creative and conscious energy that engenders awareness in matter. Also refers inclusively to the domain of existence for Transpersonal, noncorporeal consciousnesses.

Sticky One: The part of soul that is most animalistic or childlike. Playful, sensory, and emotionally and energetically sensitive. It enfolds the body in an energetic sheath that extends out about an inch around the skin. This part gathers and directs energy in magical workings. Also known as Fetch.

World: The entirety of experienced reality, which includes the Self. An immanent, conscious wholeness.

THANK YOU

This book draws upon the guidance and instruction of many potent teachers and traditions. Honor goes to the gods, Victor and Cora Anderson, T. Thorn Coyle, and many wonderful teachers in Reclaiming and the Anderson Feri/Faery traditions, particularly Jennifer Byers, River Roberts, Wolfe, Michael Foltz, Tari Follett, Scarecrow, and Dawn Isidora. Honor also goes to my past, present, and future colleagues in Morningstar Mystery School, whose work teaches and inspires me.

Thank you to Niki Whiting for reviewing a draft of this book and providing excellent feedback. Thank you to Casandra Johns, who did kick-ass copyediting. Thank you to Rhyd Wildermuth, who has been a great friend and a champion of my writing.

I am so thankful for my husband Jack, who has given me love, support, the occasional needed kick in the ass, sweet kisses, great cooking, the opportunity to build a home, and hours of his handsome face. I am thankful for Dan, who has taught me how to love even more deeply.

I am thankful for the friends who have been in my heart throughout work on this book: Evan, Woods, Andrea, and Matthew. Gratitude to Billy for being willing to take a step that opened up my life.

I am deeply thankful to my family, who has loved and supported me unflinchingly throughout my life. Though we have grown in different directions and I am no longer in the religion or political ideology in which I was raised, I feel that I am still grounded in the values they taught me.

About The Author

Anthony Rella is a witch, writer, and therapist in Seattle, Washington. He has been a spiritual seeker his entire life, a tarot reader since one drunken night in college, and a practicing witch most of his adult life. He began studying and practicing in the Reclaiming tradition in Chicago in 2004, and became actively involved in building community and running public rituals during the subsequent three years. He also became an initiate of the tradition now known as Fellowship of the Phoenix, and has supported the group in building its Seattle temple. In 2006, Anthony began studying Feri witchcraft with T. Thorn Coyle, and continued studying with her as her work evolved into Morningstar Mystery School. Anthony is a student, teacher, and occasional committee member in Morningstar, and holds the Blue, White, and Gold cords of the School.

Anthony has been working full-time as a mental health counselor for 2013, spending three years in community mental health until moving full-time into private practice. Anthony's counseling experience includes work with LGBTQ people, homeless youth and adults, people with chronic mental illness, and people with criminal charges—engaging in deferred sentencing, on probation, under correctional supervision, or transitioning out of incarceration.

About Gods& Radicals Press

On the first of May, 2015, Gods&Radicals began, bearing a banner of tree and fist. Holding in our hands the threads of anarchist, Marxist, anti-colonialist, druidic, feminist, occult, environmentalist, and esoteric thought, we began a dance around a center constantly plaiting, constantly weaving in fierce celebration of all that makes the world beautiful and all that we refuse to let be taken from us. We know the power of mead and molotov, the beauty of ancient forest and shattered window, the sacred celebration of spiral dance and protest march. We speak in the quiet whispers of conspiracy and graveyard, swim in the currents of tumultuous ocean and political dissent, and read the future in the bones of animals and the pale faces of politicians.

Circling the Star is our eighth book.
Our other titles include
Curse Your Boss, Hex The State, Take Back The World, by Dr. Bones
Pagan Anarchism, by Christopher Scott Thompson
A Pagan Anti-Capitalist Primer, by Alley Valkyrie & Rhyd Wildermuth
A Beautiful Resistance: The Crossing
A Beautiful Resistance: Left Sacred
A Beautiful Resistance: The Fire Is Here
A Beautiful Resistance: Everything We Already Are

For ordering information, see our online bookstore at
ABeautifulResistance.com
or visit our website and online journal at:
GodsAndRadicals.Org

www.ingramcontent.com/pod-product-compliance
Lightning Source LLC
Chambersburg PA
CBHW070427010526
44118CB00014B/1929